A
Colonial Plantation
Cookbook

D1636286

A Colonial Plantation Cookbook:

The Receipt Book of Harriott Pinckney Horry, 1770

*Edited with an
Introduction by*
RICHARD J. HOOKER

UNIVERSITY OF SOUTH CAROLINA PRESS

Frontispiece: Harriott Pinckney Horry, 1748–1830; a miniature attributed to Walter Robertson *(Courtesy of Amherst College and the Frick Art Reference Library).*

Published in Columbia, South Carolina, by the University of South Carolina Press

First Edition

Manufactured in the United States of America

Library of Congress Cataloging in Publication Data

Horry, Harriott Pinckney, 1748–1830.
  A colonial plantation cookbook.

  Includes bibliographical references and index.
  1. Cookery, American.   I. Hooker, Richard James,
1913–   . II. Title.
TX703.H67   1984   641.5973   84-12016
ISBN 0-87249-437-3

To Nancy

Contents

Introduction

In 1770 a young South Carolina woman, recently married, wrote her name and the date on the first page of a book of blank pages. In this way Harriott Horry began a cookbook which, by the common practice of the time, she called a receipt book. The work, which came to contain mostly recipes and also some household directions, reveals much about the eating and drinking habits of her time and place, but also something about Harriott herself, her world of the South Carolina lowlands, and the lives of the rice and indigo planters, merchants, and lawyers who made up the colony's elite. There are also glimpses of the work on the beautiful Hampton plantation where Harriott lived for over sixty years—its kitchen, dairy and smokehouse, the dying of homespun cloths, defense against insects, the preserving of foods, the care of valued trees, the painting of the plantation house and outbuildings, and even such homely tasks as washing silk stockings, making soap, preparing hair dressings, or washing carpets.

Her receipt book and other writings show Harriott to have been intelligent, capable, perceptive, hard-working, and charming. In all these ways she resembled her mother, Eliza Lucas Pinckney, who had done much to mold her character. To understand Harriott one must know something of this remarkable woman.

Eliza Lucas had been born to English parents in the West Indies about 1722, had attended school in England, returned briefly to Antigua where her father was an officer in the British army, and then at the age of fifteen accompanied her parents to a plantation on Wappoo Creek, near Charles Town, South Carolina. When her father had to go back to Antigua in 1739 Eliza, aged seventeen, took over management of this plantation and supervision of two others, for her mother was sickly.

Highly intelligent and filled with joy at life's opportunities, Eliza took on numerous projects: teaching two slave children to read so that they might become school mistresses to the others; practicing her French and shorthand regularly; learning some law and helping her neighbors write their wills; and, daily, reading in a small library and devoting time to "my darling amusement Musick." Owning that she loved "the vegitable world extremly," she began a large fig orchard and planned a cedar grove to be filled with all kinds of wild and cultivated flowers and fruit trees. There was also to be a large oak plantation to provide timbers for future British fleets, with the profits to go to charity.[1]

Eliza also experimented with the seeds of various plants sent from Antigua by her father, who had become lieutenant-governor there. After overcoming many problems with indigo she finally produced a successful crop and in 1744 distributed seeds to other planters.[2] Although she was not the first South Carolinian to raise indigo, it was a remarkable accomplishment for a young girl in her time and place.

In the same year Eliza married Charles Pinckney, a well-to-do widower, attorney, prominent political leader, and to be briefly the chief justice of South Carolina. The couple soon had three children who lived, two sons and Harriott who was born in 1748. The brothers, Charles Cotesworth and Thomas, were to become outstanding men in state and national affairs—military, political, and diplomatic.

1. *The Letterbook of Eliza Lucas Pinckney, 1739–1762,* ed. by Elise Pinckney (Chapel Hill, 1972), pp. 7, 34–38, 41.

2. Harriott Horry Ravenel, *Eliza Pinckney* (New York, 1896), pp. 102–7; Frances Leigh Williams, *A Founding Family: the Pinckneys of South Carolina* (New York, 1978), pp. 10–12.

The family moved to England in 1753 where the two boys were placed in school. It was not until May 1758 that the parents and Harriott returned to South Carolina where Charles Pinckney soon died. Eliza Pinckney took up management of the plantations and, in her deep grief, concentrated on the education of Harriott.

Eliza's letters give some picture of the girl. Harriott was of a lively disposition, growing tall (Eliza herself was rather short), fluent in French, and attracted to books. She was also, Eliza wrote, fond of learning "and I shall indulge her in it." In 1762 Eliza confessed that attention to Harriott was "one of the great Businesses of my life," and that to teach "a mind so tractable and a temper so sweet" was a pleasure. Harriott was presently engaged, she added, in geography and music.[3] One can be sure that she also received a thorough grounding in household duties and the complexities of plantation management.

A portrait, which no longer exists, showed Harriott at eighteen to have been pretty, slender, of good height, and with blue eyes and curly blonde hair. In February 1768, she married Daniel Horry, a widower about sixteen years older than she. Horry was of a wealthy Huguenot family that had settled early in Car-

---

3. *Letterbook of Eliza Pinckney,* pp. 35–49.

olina's history on the lower Santee River. He owned many rice plantations along that river and lived in one of them, the beautiful Hampton,[4] though each spring the Horrys moved to their large house on the corner of Broad and Legare streets in Charles Town to escape the summer fevers. They very likely went there in late winter too, for it was then that the South Carolina elite, just forming, gathered to enjoy balls, dinners, and horse races. The inhabitants of Charles Town, wrote Eliza, are "polite and live in a very gentile manner."[5]

Daniel Horry, like many South Carolinians, had a passion for horse racing, an addiction that Harriott accepted as a "manly amusement." Harriott herself probably entered into various plantation activities early. Soon after her daughter's marriage, Eliza wrote to Daniel Horry that "I am glad your little wife looks well

4. For a description of Hampton Plantation, with illustrations, see Archibald Rutledge, *Home by the River* (Indianapolis, 1951). An account of the area in which Hampton was located, and of the production of rice there, is in G. S. S., "Sketches of the South Santee," *American Monthly Magazine,* 8 (October, November 1836):313–19, 431–42, as given in Eugene L. Schwaab (ed.), *Travels in the Old South* (n.p. 1973), pp. 4ff.

5. Ravenel, *Eliza Pinckney,* p. 18. For an excellent account of Charleston during roughly the period that Harriott lived there see George C. Rogers, Jr., *Charleston in the Age of the Pinckneys* (Columbia, S.C., 1980).

to the ways of her home (or housework). I dare say she will not eat the bread of Idleness which she is able to do otherwise. . . . The management of a Dairy is an amusement she has been always fond of, and 'tis a very useful one, I will answer for it, hers is perfectly neat."[6] The management of the kitchen would also have been hers, and two years after her marriage she began a cookbook. Already she had had a son and soon afterwards a daughter.

During the War of Independence Harriott suffered privations, worry, and loss of property to British raids. Her husband fought the British as a colonel of dragoons until after Charles Town fell. Then, when the British overran the Santee area he, possibly fearful for his wife and family, "took protection" from the British and soon afterwards sailed for England to place his son in school there.[7] Harriott remained at Hampton to manage the various plantations as best she could in wartime. The plantation became a place of refuge for friends who fled the British occupation of Charles Town and elsewhere, and at one time twenty-six were there.[8]

---

6. Eliza Lucas Pinckney to Daniel Horry, Mar. 7, 1768, South Carolina Historical Society. This is referred to hereinafter as the SCHS.

7. Williams, *A Founding Family,* pp. 39, 86, 95, 135–36, 160.

8. Rutledge, *Home by the River,* p. 53.

Horry returned to South Carolina in March 1782, but nearly lost his plantations as a loyalist and did have to suffer a twelve percent amercement on his entire estate. In November 1785, Horry died at Hampton of a fever.[9] Harriott's two brothers had played outstanding roles as officers during the war, and Harriott's own feelings were almost certainly supportive of the American cause.

Following the death of her husband, Harriott, aided by her mother who had come to live with her, took over full management of the plantations. These presumably did well, for in 1786 Harriott went to the considerable expense of ordering a coach from London. She and her mother knew a day of glory in 1791 when President Washington stopped at Hampton for breakfast and remained to dine,[10] a visit probably intended as an acknowledgment of the considerable role played by the Pinckney brothers in the recent war. Two years after this visit Harriott accompanied her mother, a cancer victim, to Philadelphia in search of medical aid, where Eliza died. After an interval of

---

9. Williams, *A Founding Family*, p. 210; George C. Rogers, Jr., *The History of Georgetown County, South Carolina* (Columbia, 1970), p. 160 and note.

10. A. S. Salley, *President Washington's Tour Through South Carolina in 1791* (Bulletin of the Historical Commission of South Carolina, No. 12) (Columbia, 1932), p. 8.

mourning, Harriott continued her travels through some of the northern states. In 1815 she made another extensive trip northward. Ten years later she was honored by a visit from Lafayette, whose niece had married Harriott's son, during his American tour.[11] Harriott, like her mother and two brothers, had a long life, not dying until 1830.

That Harriott was interested in foods, beverages, and kitchen management appears clearly in her cookbook, for there she not only gathered numerous recipes with careful attention to details, but evaluated and changed some recipes and at times substituted "better" ones for those she had found unsatisfactory. Her journals of trips to more northern states in 1793 and 1815 provide more evidence.

The first of these expeditions began after the death of her mother in Philadelphia and lasted from June to the following December. Harriott was accompanied by her daughter Harriott together with Maria and Harriott Pinckney, daughters of her brother Charles Cotesworth Pinckney. At all times Harriott observed farms and dairies with an experienced eye and commented on the meals taken with friends or enjoyed at good taverns and endured at poor ones.

---

11. Mrs. St. Julien Ravenel, *Charleston: the Place and the People* (New York, 1912), pp. 392, 445; Williams, *A Founding Family,* pp. 292–94; Journals of Harriott Horry, 1793, 1815, SCHS.

The party first set out to visit Bethlehem, Pennsylvania, and Harriott noted the fields of wheat, barley, oats, flax, hay, Irish potatoes, rye, clover, and Indian corn on the way, as well as cherry orchards. At Craig's tavern they were given "tough fowles and stewed veal." In Bethlehem itself, founded about fifty years earlier by the United Brethren (commonly called Moravians), Harriott saw the women's kitchen where everything was arranged so that two women could cook for one hundred and thirty "Sisters," but all was either boiled in six iron kettles or baked in a very large oven. At Nazareth, not far away, she saw Moravians brewing beer, distilling rye whiskey, the cider press, the dairy, and flour mill.

Returning to Philadelphia the party ate at Moore's tavern in Jenkintown where everything was "neat" as possible: "The cleanliness and brightness of the kitchen and every thing in it exceeded every house I have seen." In the kitchen Harriott was shown a stove which Mrs. Moore called a ten plate stove and on which she said she cooked everything. Harriott's interest was justifiable, for the iron stove, just then in its infancy, would in the next century greatly change cooking methods and relieve women from the drudgery of fireplace cooking.[12] Moving northward, Harriott dined at Mowers tav-

---

12. Richard J. Hooker, *Food and Drink in America: A History* (New York, 1981), pp. 95–96.

ern in Worcester, Massachusetts, where she had "one of the best dinners we have met with." In Connecticut she saw many cider presses along the road as well as fine quince trees. Going south again the travelers visited the dairy of one Mrs. Rutherford in Tranquility, New Jersey, where, Harriott wrote, "the best Cheese in America is made." Once more in Bethlehem the travelers attended a Moravian Love Feast where coffee and cakes were served, and at Olivers tavern in Virginia they ate of "2 tough Turkeys and as tough pork."[13]

On the 1815 expedition Harriott was accompanied by her daughter, Mrs. Martin, an intimate friend, and her brother Thomas Pinckney. A stop on the Pee Dee River was in a large, new house "and were it not for Bugs and feather Bags, tough fowles and knives that would not cut" the visit was rated "good for Pedee." At Warrington, North Carolina, the group put up at one Ruffins and the heat of the day "made us relish the ice which was immediately handed to us and a bottle of Cyder." After crossing the Roanoke they dined at one Gohlsons "(on pig and pork and Bacon)," but in a new clean home with an ice house.

Richmond, Virginia, was more interesting. There they were able to get rooms at the home of Mary Randolph, who would nine years later

---

13. Harriott Horry, Journal, 1793, SCHS.

publish *The Virginia House-wife: or Methodical Cook,*[14] an outstanding work that would in numerous editions influence American cookery considerably, both by its excellent recipes and by its inclusion of many American dishes and ingredients. Mary Randolph had opened her boardinghouse in 1808 and continued it until 1819. Witty, charming, and providing outstanding meals, she attracted a large following of wealthy and fashionable people.[15] At her home Harriott found "excellent fare and genteel treatment," but what most intrigued her was a refrigerator. This was an outward box of 4 by 3½ feet, inside which was another box four inches smaller, both made very tight and the space between filled with powdered charcoal. Harriott both sketched the wonder and wrote a detailed description. Each day Mrs. Randolph placed in the refrigerator five pecks of ice brought to her door for fifty cents and was thereby able to refrigerate for twenty-four hours pans of butter, meats, and other foods. The use of ice for the preservation of food was just beginning to reveal its revolutionary potential. Charleston had not had an ice depot

---

14. Washington, 1824.

15. Sterling P. Anderson, Jr., "Queen Molly and *The Virginia Housewife,*" *Virginia Cavalcade,* 20 (1971):33–34; Samuel Mordecais, *Richmond in By-Gone Days* (Richmond, 1856), pp. 96–99; Jane Carson, *Colonial Virginia Cookery* (Williamsburg, 1968), pp. xxxi–xxxv.

until 1799 when a hotelkeeper opened one.[16] Harriott was also interested in Mrs. Randolph's table fan. Though she had seen many, she told her journal, this one kept away flies and cooled the table so easily that "I insert it here."[17]

While in Richmond Harriott dined at the home of one Major Gibbons where Richard Channing Moore, recently appointed Bishop of Virginia in the Protestant Episcopal Church, and others were guests and had a "very nice dinner," the contents of which she listed: "the fattest" green goose, ham, tongue, cauliflower, potato, salads, peas, French beans, sturgeon, chickens, and a fine loin veal, followed by two large dishes of ice cream, strawberries, pudding, preserved gooseberries, and white heart cherries. On their travels again, the group ate at an inn near Fredericksburg where a "nice dinner" was given them of ham, fried chicken, and a quarter of lamb. In Washington the travelers saw the ruins of the Capitol and the White House, both recently burned by the British during the War of 1812.

Baltimore proved as exciting as had Richmond. Here the group put up at the Indian Queen Hotel kept by a man named Gadsby. In this "very large establishment" Harriott counted seventy to eighty places set at the com-

16. Hooker, *Food and Drink,* pp. 66, 101–2.
17. Harriott Horry, Journal, 1815, SCHS.

mon table plus many private tables. In the kitchen she noted that all the boiling was done by steam and the roasting at large open fireplaces that used spits turned by smokejacks. Similarly powered was a coffee roaster, a very large cylinder that she guessed held twenty or thirty pounds of coffee, a beverage in the early stages of a meteoric rise in popularity in America.[18] The kitchen at Gadsby's also contained a large patent oven and some stoves set in brickwork. At two private homes in Baltimore Harriott noticed especially the ice creams and strawberries included in the dessert course.

Passing through Delaware the party found that veal steaks were "the fashion" everywhere. The countryside around Lancaster, Pennsylvania, entranced Harriott with its beautiful farms and fields of wheat, rye, flax, corn, barley, oats, and clover. She saw an abundance of cherry and apple trees, but few peach trees and those bearing poorly. Always interested in dairying, Harriott found that the cows gave only from four to five gallons of milk daily contrary to stories she had heard. But she rated the butter excellent everywhere, and it was generally served with a cake of ice upon it.

Going on to New York, Harriott discovered that salmon, trout, bass, and other fish were taken from Lake George, "but I have tasted

18. Hooker, *Food and Drink,* pp. 92–93, 130.

none to equal our Santee fish." In Vermont she admired the wild mountain raspberries as beautiful and finer than any cultivated ones she had ever seen, though of less pronounced flavor. In New Hampshire, Harriott decided that the "common" food of the poor was rye and corn bread, with but very little wheat being eaten and that coarse.[19]

On her plantation or in her Charleston home, Harriott would not have lacked for good foods and drinks. At Hampton she had gardens, poultry, and livestock together with game and seafood from the nearby fields and rivers. In Charleston there were certainly a kitchen garden, a poultry yard, very likely a cow or two,[20] the daily market, and a wealth of imported delicacies from the West Indies and Europe. What either Hampton or the Charleston home might need that the other had posed no problem, for the two were not far apart by water, the customary means of travel between them.

The foods available within South Carolina were uneven in quantity and quality. Milk and

19. Harriott Horry, Journal, 1815, SCHS.

20. Livestock could be kept in Charleston. In 1798 the sexton of St. Michael's Church was directed "not to suffer any horses or cattle to graze in the Church yard in the future." George W. Williams, *St. Michael's, Charleston, 1751–1951* (Columbia, 1951), p. 181.

cheese were generally lacking except to the well-to-do. The pork and barnyard fowls, fed on corn and rice, were rated good, but the beef, veal, and mutton were but "middling" or inferior because, said one man, the cattle and sheep were not fattened but rather slaughtered direct from the thin pastures.[21] From nearby fields and waters, however, there was a plentiful supply of venison, wild turkeys, geese, ducks, and other wild fowl. Terrapin were found in all the ponds, and at times ships arrived from the West Indies with huge sea turtles. Fish were often scarce and expensive, but oysters, crabs, and shrimp could be bought cheaply.[22]

Vegetables were available in season and were preserved for the winter months. Travelers noticed that the "long" (sweet) potatoes were a great favorite and there were also white potatoes, pumpkins, various peas and beans, squashes, cucumbers, radishes, turnips, carrots, and parsnips among other vegetables.[23]

21. Journal of Lord Adam Gordon, 1764–1765, in Newton D. Mereness, ed., *Travels in the American Colonies* (New York, 1916), p. 400; J. D. Schoepf, *Travels in the Confederation* (Philadelphia, 1911), 2:189.

22. Ibid.; *A Short Description of the Province of South Carolina in the Year 1763* (London, 1770), in B. R. Carroll, *Historical Collections of South Carolina* (New York, 1836), 2:481.

23. Ibid.; Isaac Weld, *Travels through the States of North America . . . 1795, 1796 & 1797* (London, 1799),

Rice was the colony's great staple and it was served with meats and shellfish and used to make breads, biscuits, flour, puddings, and cakes. Josiah Quincy, Junior, a visitor from New England in 1773, saw at one country seat "a prodigious rice pudding made of what they call rice flour."[24] Corn served all classes to make Journey cakes and the great and small hominy. Wheat was grown by some of the Germans in the interior, but better grades were imported from Pennsylvania and New York.[25]

Lowcountry dwellers grew and enjoyed a profusion of fruits: oranges, peaches, citrons, pomegranates, lemons, pears, apples, figs, melons, nectarines, and apricots, as well as a variety of berries. "Strawberries are over, and the raspberries begin to ripen," wrote Hariott to her brother one early June.[26]

Wealthy planters and merchants were not limited to locally produced foods. From northern colonies came apples, white potatoes, and

---

p. 142; Schoepf, *Travels,* p. 189; Lewis C. Gray, *History of Agriculture in the Southern United States to 1860* (New York, 1941), 1:58.

24. "Journal of Josiah Quincy, Junior, 1773," Massachusetts Historical Society *Collections,* 49 (1915–16):443.

25. Ibid.; Julia Cherry Spruill, *Women's Life and Work in the Southern Colonies* (Chapel Hill, 1938), p. 277.

26. Gray, *History Agriculture in Southern U.S.,* 1:190–91; Harriott Horry, Letterbook 1786–1787, SCHS.

wheat, all of a better quality than those grown in South Carolina, as well as butter, cheeses, cabbages, onions, and corned beef. The West Indies, the Spanish and Portuguese islands, and Europe sent cheeses, salad oils, almonds, chocolate, olives, pimentos, raisins, sugar, limes, lemons, currants, spices, anchovies, and salt. Boats arrived in Charles Town frequently from the West Indies with many kinds of tropical fruits.[27]

As for beverages, only the slaves, the poorest whites, and hard-pressed frontiersmen drank water. The average South Carolinian more likely drank a mixture of rum and water, spruce beer, or cider, and in frontier areas peach brandy and, increasingly, whiskey as well. The more favored classes fared better with cider from New England, punch (immensely popular throughout the colonies), shrub, brandies, cordials, ratafias, claret "and other wines of the French, Spanish, or Portugal vintages" as one man noted. Madeira was the great favorite. Josiah Quincy found the wines at one private home "excellent," and at another "the richest" he had ever tasted. From Europe, too,

27. Spruill, *Women's Life and Work,* pp. 276–77; William Bartram, *Travels through North & South Carolina, Georgia, East & West Florida,* ed. Francis Harper (New Haven, 1958), pp. 13–14; Gray, *History Agriculture in Southern U.S.,* 1:58; Schoepf, *Travels,* p. 189; Ravenel, *Eliza Pinckney,* pp. 17, 47.

came beer in casks and bottles, as well as all varieties of tea.[28]

A family's larder was frequently enriched through the pleasant custom of sending to friends or relatives gifts of delicacies or even, if from the country to Charles Town, of more common foods. Thus Eliza noted that Harriott already had some "Pine-apple Cheese," but asked her to accept some turtle and fine limes. The bananas and oranges, she added, were not good enough to send. At another time she sent Harriott some pickled oysters. Eliza acknowledged receiving from Hampton turkeys, fowls, and eggs. Harriott thanked a "dear cousin" for a gift of rose water and sent in return a recipe for cheese.[29]

With a background that personally or indirectly included the West Indies, England, and South Carolina, what were the sources of Harriott's recipes? To a great degree she followed the forms of the Anglo-American upper classes. Both Eliza and her daughter had moved among the wealthy and aristocratic English, and Har-

28. Hooker, *Food and Drink,* pp. 36–37, 82–85; Journal of Lord Adam Gordon in Mereness, *Travels,* p. 400; *A Short Description of S. C.,* in Carroll, *Historical Collections,* 2:481; "Journal of Josiah Quincy," Mass. Hist. Soc. *Collections,* 49 (1915–16):442–48.

29. Ravenel, *Eliza Pinckney,* pp. 253, 255–56, 260; Harriott Horry, Letterbook, 1786–1787, SCHS.

riott in Charles Town had, as a close friend of Lady Charles Montagu, the governor's wife, needed to defend herself against the charge of being "fonder of people of Quality, than of others of Merit."[30]

The diet of Harriott and her friends was obliquely influenced by French cookery. For centuries the English gentry and nobility had accepted French cooking as superior to their own, and by the late sixteenth century it was said that most noble families had as cooks "musicall-headed Frenchmen and strangers." English patriots, to be sure, joined in anti-Gallic effusions, rejoicing that *true* Englishmen had "no meat disguis'd with strange sauces; no straggling joynt of a sheep in the midst of a pasture of grasse; beset with sallads on every side, but solid substantial food." A play of the period was similarly nationalistic, lauding the English diet as "bread, beer, and beef, yeoman's fare; we have no kickshaws: full dishes, whole bellyfuls."[31] But the aristocracy, the object of such attacks, knew well and enjoyed the ragouts, salads, soups, fricassees, daubes, and

---

30. Ravenel, *Eliza Pinckney,* p. 232.
31. Hooker, *Food and Drink,* pp. 7–8; *Harrison's Description of England,* ed. Frederick J. Furnivall (London, 1877), 1:144; Mildred Campbell, *The English Yeoman* (New York, 1942), p. 244; Marjorie Plant, *The Domestic Life in Scotland in the Eighteenth Century* (Edinburgh, 1952), p. 81.

beef "à la mode," with flavorings that included
morels, anchovies, capers, wines, and a wide
range of spices and herbs. English cookbooks of
the seventeenth and eighteenth centuries, prepared for a very small portion of the popula-
tion, had them all, and these works guided the
wealthiest and more sophisticated English and
American cooks.

These French influences embedded in upper-
class English cooking came only slowly to
America, for few of the rich or aristocratic English chose to emigrate to the "howling wilder-
ness" of that continent during the first century
and more of settlement. In that time lower and
middle-class immigrants to America tried, not
always successfully, to maintain their un-
sophisticated English cookery in the midst of
new climates, different flora and fauna, and
often primitive living conditions.

By degrees, however, there came to exist a
body of wealthy Americans with pretensions to
social superiority. These, as best they could,
imitated the English upper classes, mingled
with the royally-appointed British officials in
the colonies, and patterned their behavior, in-
cluding their eating and drinking customs,
upon what they discovered in this close rela-
tionship or through visits to what they called
"home."

It was by then necessary, however, to accommodate deep-set American food customs. Corn,

pork, rice, pumpkins, and other American standbys, both native and imported, had become entrenched in favor. Robert Beverley, the eighteenth-century historian of Virginia, wrote that though the rich planters had wheat bread, some of them "rather choose the Pone." Virginia cured hams were a basic food in that colony. Eliza Pinckney sent some rice to the master of her children's school in England, explaining that they liked it with their meat in preference to bread. Sweet potatoes would follow, she added, when they had matured.[32]

Influences upon American cookery directly from France were slight, for not until the late seventeenth century, after France ceased its toleration of protestants, was there a small immigration of Huguenots, too few to affect greatly American cooking habits. Indeed, insofar as England and her possessions were in an almost continuous state of war with France between 1689 and 1763, anything French was likely to be looked upon with disfavor.

A sharp change took place shortly after Harriott began her cookbook. During the War of Independence the French alliance of 1778 made a friend out of an enemy and brought French troops and their officers to America. The reorientation of the upper classes that followed

---

32. Robert Beverley, *The History and Present State of Virginia,* ed. Louis B. Wright (Chapel Hill, 1947), p. 293; *Letterbook of Eliza Pinckney,* p. 97.

the alliance was expressed by John Adams who went to France in 1778 on a diplomatic mission. Within a year after his arrival he confided to Abigail that "The Cookery, and manner of living here, which you know, Americans were taught by their former absurd Masters [the English] to dislike is more agreable to me, than you can imagine."[33] The new influence grew during the French Revolution when a small stream of refugee chefs and pastry cooks came to America to open cafes, restaurants, ice cream parlors, and pastry shops. Soon, too, there were skilled cooks among the French refugees from the slave revolts in Santo Domingo.[34]

But many of Harriott's recipes were wholly or largely of American origin. The various recipes for curing bacon (hams) would fall in this category, as would probably those for stewing crabs, stewing ducks, sausage, pickled shrimps, journey cake, biscuits, rice milk, pap pudding, yam pudding, apple pudding, rice pie, one of the rice bread recipes, baked pears, pumpkin chips, water cake, spruce beers, preserved quinces, preserved peaches, raspberry bran-

33. John Adams to Abigail Adams, Passy, Feb. 21, 1779, *The Book of Abigail and John: Selected Letters of the Adams Family, 1762–1784,* ed. by L. H. Butterfield, Marc Friedlaender and Mary-Jo Kline (Cambridge, Mass., 1975), p. 240.

34. Hooker, *Food and Drink,* pp. 76–80.

dies, and plum brandy among others. The coconut puffs, the recipe to caveach fish, and the rum punches may well have come from the West Indies.

It has often been said that there are no new recipes. While this is an exaggeration, it is true that at any given time the vast majority of recipes come from preceding generations and will, with the sources rarely acknowledged, be taken over by succeeding ones. In passage they may, of course, be rendered faulty by improper copying, improved by skilled cooks, or adjusted to accommodate new ingredients or new techniques of food preparation.

Harriott's book, with its one hundred and twenty-four recipes for foods and drinks, reveals strikingly this continuity of recipes from generation to generation. Her mother, Eliza Lucas Pinckney, had prepared in 1756 a small collection of recipes and of cures for illnesses.[35] Many of her recipes had been acquired from American and English friends and among the latter, especially, were some that had very likely been passed down, little changed, from the seventeenth and early eighteenth centuries. Two recipes had been reworked, with

35. Eliza Lucas Pinckney receipt book, on deposit by the Colonial Dames of America in the State of South Carolina in the Library of the SCHS.

few changes, from ones in a popular English work by Hannah Glasse.[36]

Harriott chose twenty-six recipes from her mother's collection to put into her own, very likely those she had enjoyed especially as a child and young woman. Some were copied nearly word for word while others showed modifications of language, ingredients, or techniques, evidence that Harriott was alert to the problems of cookery. Those chosen were, as Harriott listed them in her table of contents:

To Pott Beef like
    Venison
To Dobe a Rump
    of Beef
Beef Collops
Stewed
    Mushrooms
To Caveach Fish
Snow Cream
Baked Pares
Yam Pudding
Little Puddings
Mince Pyes
Rusks
Mushroom
    Catchup and
    powder
Queen Sauce

Black Caps
Plumb
    Marmalade
Orange
    Marmalade
Almond Cream
Coco Nut Puffs
Cheese Cakes
Egg Pyes
Orange Pudding
Rennet
Pickle for Hams,
    Tongues or
    Dutch Beef
Ratifia
Orange Flower
    Ratifia
Duke of Norfolk
    Punch

36. [Hannah Glasse], *The Art of Cookery, Made Plain and Easy* . . . . (London, 1747).

The other recipes in Harriott's collection came from a variety of sources. Several were from printed works, a good number were from friends and were so acknowledged, and a few were Harriott's own. Finally, it is likely that some came from the Horry family's recipes and were of French Huguenot origin. Candidates for this category would include that for dressing a calf's head, the white fricassee, the brown fricassee, the ragout of breast of veal, the stewed pigeons, and the preserved tomatoes, though similar recipes could be found in English cookbooks of the time.

If Harriott borrowed, so was she borrowed from. In 1847, seventeen years after Harriott's death, Sarah Rutledge, the daughter of Edward Rutledge, a signer of the Declaration of Independence, published *The Carolina Housewife, or House and Home,* a large collection of recipes which she had gathered from friends and acquaintances.[37] This work contained twenty-one recipes from Harriott's book, though some were so changed in wording as to suggest that they might have come indirectly from that work. Sarah Rutledge would have known Harriott. As a child Sarah had been taken to England for schooling by Thomas Pinckney, Harriott's brother, along with his own children,

---

37. There have been various editions of this work, the latest a facsimile of the 1847 edition with an introduction by Anna Wells Rutledge (Columbia, S.C., 1979).

and later in Charleston Harriott and Sarah would have known each other for about four decades.[38]

At least three of the recipes taken by Sarah Rutledge from Harriott's book were ones that Harriott had taken from her mother's work: "To Pott Beef like Venison," "To Dobe a Rump of Beef," and "To Caveach Mackrel." The first and third of these long-lived recipes had come to Eliza from Hannah Glasse's cookbook of the mid-eighteenth century.

In her choice of flavorings, as in her selection of recipes, Harriott largely followed upper class Anglo-American practices. About 1770 Martha Bradley, the compiler of an English cookbook, noted that the principal spices used in England were cloves, mace, nutmegs, cinnamon, ginger, pepper, and allspice.[39] Harriott made liberal use of all of these, with nutmeg, mace, pepper and cloves used most often, and allspice, cinnamon, and ginger less frequently. Employed at least once were saffron, carraway seeds, turmeric, China roots, sassafras, cayenne pepper, bay leaf, mustard seed, sage, and sago leaves. "Sweet herbs" and shallots were frequently

---

38. The two were connected by marriage, most closely by the marriage of Harriott's brother Charles Cotesworth Pinckney to Sarah Middleton, a sister of Sarah Rutledge's mother.

39. Martha Bradley, *The British Housewife* . . . . (n.p., [1770?]), p. 11.

called for and, less often, horseradish, marjoram, thyme, parsley, and garlic. The last was used only in pickling and preserving, for the English, and the Americans after them, had given up this herb for salads and cooking, labeling it rank-smelling and generally undesirable.[40] Harriott followed English practices, too, in using both rosewater and orange flower water.

Quite a few of Harriott's recipes call for a lavish use of butter, milk, and cream. This was also in line with English practices, though only a few South Carolinians would have had the ingredients to work with. But Hampton in 1772 had forty cows,[41] and Harriott had made supervision of the dairy a special interest, contributing to her book the essay on "Making Butter," the method "to preserve Butter," and a means of sweetening butter made from the milk of cows that had eaten too well of turnip flowers.

A major and constant problem faced by Harriott, like all in that pre-refrigeration age, was in preserving foods. In South Carolina the low-country summers were very hot and winter temperatures rarely fell to freezing. Thus many of Harriott's recipes were for preserving,

40. See John Evelyn, *Acetaria: A Discourse of Sallets* (London, 1699), p. 27; C. Anne Wilson, *Food & Drink in Britain* (London, 1973), p. 361.

41. Will of Daniel Horry (perhaps a contemporary copy), July 2, 1772, South Carolina Archives.

pickling, smoking, salting, drying, and curing
of both meats and vegetables, and the making
of jellies, marmalades, and sausages. She had a
recipe to caveach mackerel ("They will keep
well cover'd a great while and are delicious"), to
keep tomatoes for winter use, to corn beef, and
four different methods to cure hams or bacon,
two of them from Virginia whose reputation for
hams was already well established. Like English cooks of her day, Harriott showed a
fondness for marmalades, for with these one
could capture for winter days some of the color
and taste of summer.

Also English was a devotion to puddings. By
the 1740s these were described in England as
"so necessary a part of an Englishman's food"
that with beef they were held "the victuals they
most love." Harriott had ten puddings in her
book of the sweet, baked variety suitable for
desserts, rather than the boiled puddings,
heavy the suet, that had long served the English as first course fillers.[42] She also had three
creams, a "Blanc Manger," and numerous
other desserts. A devotion to sweet dishes, encouraged by easy access to cheap sugar and molasses from the West Indies, had become a
characteristic of the American diet.[43]

Harriott's book has eleven recipes for bev-

---

42. Hooker, *Food and Drink,* pp. 3, 7, 40, 41, 122.
43. Ibid., pp. 33–34, 62–63, 121–25.

erages to supplement what would have been the periodical imports of rum from the West Indies, cider from New England and New York, beers from England, and wines from Europe and the Spanish and Portuguese islands. The spruce beers, the shrubs, the cordials, and the common punches were certainly for daily use, while the Duke of Norfolk Punch would have been for a very large party.

The recipes in Harriott's book could not have been a cross section of those intended for the Horry table. There would have been many simple, everyday dishes that would not need inclusion—soups, salads, additional corn and rice dishes, seafoods, pickles, and so on.

Harriott began her book in 1770 and so dated it, but she added from time to time to her original collection of recipes. Though her handwriting remained firm throughout the book, showing none of the shakiness that often accompanies an advanced age, there are other means of separating the earlier from the later recipes. The order in which the recipes were listed in each category of the table of contents is useful, for one can certainly assume that the first given were the earliest. In these first listings the page sequence was orderly, whereas later additions were often placed where space was available. Among these first listings are those known to have come from Eliza Lucas Pinckney's collection together with those suspected of having been taken over from the Horry family. Recipes scattered among these are presumably dated by association.

There are other leads to a possible chronology. Thus, there is a progressive decline in Harriott's capitalizing of nouns and some verbs as there is in her dated letters and journals, leading by 1815 to virtually modern usage in this respect. Again, during the same time period certain of her letters moved toward a greater simplicity, such as the 6's, P's, and, most useful of all, the e's. In the early recipes, as in her early dated letters,[44] the e's are slanted sharply upwards. A large proportion of level e's appear in later recipes as they do in her Journal of 1793. In the Journal of 1815 the slanted e's have disappeared.

Between the earliest recipes and those that are somewhat later there appears to be a gap in the progressive changes in Harriott's handwriting. One can suspect that the eight years of the War of Independence might have been responsible, for during that conflict the niceties of cookery, and the receipt book, were probably neglected.

With what clues are available, and admitting freely the possibility of errors, one can offer a tentative chronology as follows, using Har-

---

44. See letters of Harriott Horry to Mrs. Blake, Feb. 2, 1769, and Nov. 27, 1769, SCHS.

riott's page numbers which are given in brackets within the text.

The earliest recipes, quite certainly of 1770 or very shortly afterwards, are those on pages 1 through 10, 14 through 29, 32 and 33, and the recipe for "Wigs" on page 36.

Somewhat later, possibly from the end of the War in 1783 to the end of the century, are the recipes on pages 11 through 13, 30 and 31, 34 and 35, "Water Cakes" and "Naples Biscuits" on page 36, 37 through 52, and 54. The "Rum Punch," a loose-leafed recipe at the end is also in this group.

The most recent recipes, probably added during the first two decades of the nineteenth century, include those on pages 53 and 55 through 60. The recipe on page 58 is in another hand as are three of the loose recipes at the end.

Many recipes were marked with a cross in the margin to the left of the title. In some cases there is a second cross, larger and with a lighter pen. These have been rendered by a small and a large x respectively. Did they mark recipes that were tried and found successful, or simply recipes attempted? Or could the dissimilar x's have indicated recipes made by particular slave women? Still another possibility is that they were made separately by Harriott and her mother (who long lived with her) for one of the above reasons.

The cooking at Hampton and in the Horry

home in Charles Town, as in the homes of the
well-to-do throughout the South, was of course
done by slaves, nearly always women. These
formed by far the largest body of professional
cooks in the country, and that many became
proficient cooks, and some highly sensitive,
skilled kitchen artists there can be no doubt. A
woman in Middleburg, Virginia, wrote her sister about the retention of a slave woman during the dispersal of a family estate. "She is a
fine cook," she wrote, "and there were a great
many wealthy gentlemen wanting her, said
they wouldn't stop at any price. If she had been
put up to the highest bidder, such bidding never
would have been known in this part of the
world."[45]

That the kitchen work could be divided
among a number of slaves was indicated in a
letter that Eliza Pinckney wrote to her daughter, describing either the arrangements in her
own home in Charleston or, more likely, those
at the Broad Street home of the Horrys which
she was caring for. Mary-Ann, she wrote, was
the cook and "understands roasting poultry in
the greatest perfection you ever saw." She also
made the punch. Daphne baked bread and
cooked on occasion "that she may not forget

---

45. E. N. Noland to Ella Mackenzie, Glen Ora,
Middleburg, Va., Nov. 14, 1849, Ella Noland Mackenzie
Papers, Wilson Library, University of North Carolina,
Chapel Hill.

what she learnt at Santee." Old Ebba fattened the poultry to "a nicety," while young Ebba fetched wood, water, and scoured, and was to learn as much as she could of cooking and washing.[46]

Are Harriott's recipes still usable? The answer must be yes, with some qualifications. Most could be made by anyone capable of following a recipe. Others would require some expertise, such as knowing how to meet a call for "sweet herbs" or for other herbs or spices "to tast." A few recipes would discourage nearly everyone, for only a rare individual would choose to knead biscuit dough for an hour, or to undertake an elaborate preparation of a calf's head.

---

46. Ravenel, *Eliza Pinckney*, p. 245.

Treatment of the Text

Harriott Horry's receipt book was given to the South Carolina Historical Society by Mrs. Francis B. Stewart in 1952. It has never before been published, though in 1959 some extracts from it appeared in *The South Carolina Historical Magazine*.[47]

The manuscript work is bound within a thin leather cover and measures almost exactly eight by nine inches. Within the bound volume is a quite distinct work by Harriott. Unlike her mother and innumerable others of the eighteenth and earlier centuries, Harriott separated recipes for food and drink from prescriptions for illnesses. Thus from the back page of her book, the volume turned upside down to emphasize the different character of the collection, Harriott began a compilation of sixty-one cures for the common ills of her time and place, from "Ague and Fever" to the

---

47. "Extracts from Harriott Horry's Receipt Book," *The South Carolina Historical Magazine*, 60 (1959):28–29, 106, 169, 228.

"Yaws." The editing of this work has been left to some medical historian.

Transcribing the manuscript did not offer any great problems, though in a few places it was necessary to admit, within brackets, that one or more words were illegible. No changes were made in the grammar, spelling, or capitalization. With but few exceptions the text is given as Harriott rendered it. The ampersand is given as "and," the thorn as "th," and the symbol for pound as "lb." Words abbreviated with a raised final letter have been spelled out, but contractions of words which employ the apostrophe are left in their original form.

Since Harriott's spelling is left intact a reader should be prepared for such words as past (paste), soop (soup), flower (flour), thro' (throw), tast (taste), peice (piece), as well as to-gether, pares, hott, and puding among others. Shallot appears in five different spellings.

The capitalization is erratic. Punctuation is very slight at times, though never to the point where the meaning cannot be perceived. The use of [sic] has been reserved for errors—where a word is repeated for instance—or where without such an alert the editor might be condemned as careless. Harriott's page numbers, given in brackets within the text, are of course those she uses in her table of contents and in cross-references and by the editor in footnote cross-references. The index uses the pagination of the present volume.

Hampton Plantation

Photograph courtesy of *South Carolina Wildlife Magazine*, S.C. Wildlife and Marine Resources Department

Harriott Horry 1770

Pickles and Sauces

Mushroom Catchup and powder	26
Queen Sauce	26
Walnut Catchup	26
Ats Jarr or Pucholilla	27
Mango Musk Mellons or Cucumbers	28
To keep Tomatoes for Winter use	28
Rennet	29
Pickle for Hams, Tongues or Dutch Beef	29
Yeast	30
Soap	31
Pococks Pickle	31
Fish sauce	42
French Pomatum	45
To corn Beef	46
Bacon 48. 49. 54. 55.	
Pickle Onions	

Preserve Quinces and Marmalade	35
Raspberry Jam	35
Orange Marmalade	35
Water cake	36
Butter	46 and 37
Thin Naples biscuit	36
Citron Biscuit or very light little cakes	42
Portugal cake	13
Iceing for cakes	13
Pap Pudding	13
Jumbles	43 and 48
rice Milk	37

Liquors

Ratifia	32
Orange Flower Ratifia	32
Spruce Beer	32
Duke of Norfolks Punch	33
Shrub	33
Cherry Brandy	33
Raspberry Vinegar	35
Golden Cordial	47
Raspberry Brandy	47
Vinegar	56

Paints, Dyes, Cements etc.	
Strong Cement	50 to 54
Wash carpets	51

[*The following recipes were omitted from Harriott's table of contents through error or as late acquisitions. The titles are as they appear on the recipes, and the pagination is Harriott's:*]

[The last four recipes are on loose sheets or scraps of paper. They are without page numbers.]

[Rum Punch]
To make Solid Syllabub, a nice dessert
Orange flower syrup
Kitchen Pepper

[1]   **To make good Gravy**

Take a peice of lean Beef cut in thin Peices put a peice of Butter in Your Stew Pan and fry it Brown but take care it does not Burn. Season it with Pepper, Salt, Mace and Cloves; when it becomes a little Brown thro' in a little Strong broth made of some Beef or Veal Bones, a Couple of Anchovies,[1] and a Gill of Claret, boil it up and set it by for any use in the Savory way of Cooking.

---

1. Since the seventeenth century the English had used anchovies in certain meat and salad dishes and as appetizers. A common substitute was to pickle smelts or small herrings. See Wilson, *Food and Drink,* p. 55. An early American recipe for imitation anchovies is in *Mrs. Gardiner's Receipts from 1763* (Hallowell, Maine, 1938), p. 33.

To Dress a Calves Head

Boil the head till the Tongue will Peal, then cut half the Head into small peices, about the size of an oyster, then stew it in Strong Gravy, with a large Ladle full of Claret, and a handfull of sweet herbs, a little lemon peal, a peice of Onion and Nutmeg. Let all These stew till they are tender: Take the other half of the head and boil it, scratch it across, strew over it grated Bread and sweet herbs with a little lemon Peal: Lard it with Bacon, and wash it over with the Yolks of Eggs, and strew over it a little grated Bread and Place it in the middle of your dish. Then put a pint a pint [*sic*] of strong Gravy into your stew pan with three Anchovies, a few Capers[2] a good many Mushrooms a good quantity of sweet Butter, and a quart of large Oysters; stew the Oysters in their own liquor with a Blade of Mace and a little white wine, keep the largest to fry, and shred a few of the smallest; then Beat the Yolks of Eggs [2] and Flour, dip them in and fry them in Hogs Lard, make little Cakes of the Brains and dip them in and fry them, then pour the stew'd meat in the dish with the other half of the head, and lay the fried Oysters, Brains and Tongue, with little

---

2. Imitation capers were made by preserving nasturtium blossoms in vinegar. See Prudence Smith, *Modern American Cookery*. . . . (New York, 1831), p. 83.

bits of crispt bacon, and force meat[3] Balls, on
the Top and all about the meat, garnish with
horseradish and Barberries[4] and serve it hott.

White Frigasee

x

Parboil your Chicken, then skin them and cut
them in peices and put them in a stew pan with
gravy, a blade of mace, Nutmeg, two Anchovies,
the Echalots, a little salt, whole pepper and
white wine. When they are enough take out the
Echalots and put in half a pint of good Cream, a
peice of Butter roled in flow'r and thicken it
with the Yolk of an Egg; wring in the juice of a
Lemon, but be very carefull it don't curdle.
Mushrooms, a few Capers, and Oysters fried,
and a little of their liquor if you have it. Then
serve it to the Table on Sippets.[5]

---

3. Forcemeat was finely chopped and highly seasoned
meat or fish, frequently used as stuffing.

4. The red berries of the barberry shrub, long used by
the English, grew widely in eastern North America.
They had a pleasantly agreeable acid taste. See Richard
le Strange, *A History of Herbal Plants* (New York, 1977),
p. 54.

5. Small pieces of toasted bread, called sippets, were
used to garnish dishes or to absorb the gravy.

Brown Frigasee

Take Rabbits or Chickens, season them with salt, Pepper, and a little Mace, then put half a pound of Butter in your pan,[6] Brown it, and dredge it with flower; cut up your Chickens put them in and fry them Brown and have ready a quart of good strong gravy, Oysters, Mushrooms, three Anchovies a chalot or two, a bunch of sweet herbs, and a glass of Claret. [3] Season it high, and when they are boil'd enough take out the herbs, Chalots and Anchovies Bones, shred a lemon small and put in, and when your Chickens are almost brown enough, put them in and let them stew altogether keeping them shaking all the time its on the fire, and when it is as thick as cream, take it up and have ready to lay over it some Bitts of crispt Bacon, Fry Oysters in Hogs lard to make them look Brown, dip them in the Yolks of Eggs and Flour, and a little grated Nutmeg; and Forcemeat Balls: Garnish with Lemon and flowers and serve it.

---

6. The wealthy of England used butter lavishly during the seventeenth and eighteenth centuries, as did the Dutch, and Americans continued the practice. See Wilson, *Food and Drink*, p. 182; Hooker, *Food and Drink*, pp. 4, 7, 40, 57–58, 61.

Scots Collops[7]

χ

Take a Leg of Veal cut off as much into thin slices as you think will make a dish. Beat it with your rowling Pin, scratch it with a knife, Lard it with Lemon Peele, Bacon, and Thyme: then take sweet Marjoram, savory, Parsley, young Onions, Pepper, Salt, and a little Nutmeg. Chop them fine, and rub the Meat well with them. Fry them in a little fresh Butter, when they are fried enough take them out of the Pan and have ready a little strong Gravy, and dissolve some Anchovies in it, a glass of Claret, a Chalot or two a Lemon wrung in it and some lemon peele shred, let it stew between two dishes, and beat a peice of Butter with the Yolk of an Egg and thicken it up and pour it over your meat, with Crispt Bacon, fried Oysters, Mushrooms, Veal Sweet Bread pulld in little Peices, and forced meat Balls. Garnish with Horse radish and Barberries. Serve it——

---

7. Collops, a British term, were slices of meat. The word Scots has nothing to do with Scotland but rather refers to the scotching or the tenderizing of meat, in this case by beating it. For a collop recipe contemporary to that above see Catharine Brooks, *The Complete English Cook* . . . . (London, 1762), p. 39.

Beef Alamode

Take a peice of Fleshy Beef, (the round or thick Flank) take out the fat and Skin, and coarse; Then Beat it well and flatt it with the rowling pin or Cleaver, lard it with fat Bacon, quite through as long as your Meat is deep and as big as your finger, then season it high with Pepper, Salt, Cloves, Mace, and beaten Nutmeg, then put it into a Pot where nothing but Beef has been Boil'd in good strong Gravey, and put in a handfull of sweet herbs, a Bay leaf and Charlots, so let it boil till it's tender, then put in a Pint of Claret, three Anchovies, and let them stew till you find the liquor tast well and the Meat is tender, (if there is more liquor than sufficient to make an End of stewing take out the Overplus before you put in the Wine and other things) then put all the things in and let it stew till you see the liquor to thicken, and tast well of the spice, then take it up and take out the Bay leaves and Chalots; You may eat it hot or cold.

Collar'd Beef [8]

χ

Take the Gristles out of a flank of Beef, and
skin off the inside, then take two Ounces of Salt
Peter,[9] three Ozs. Bay salt, half a pound of
Common Salt, and a quarter of a pound of
Brown Sugar; Mix these all well to-gether and
rub the Beef well, and put it into a pan with a
quart of Spring Water, for four days, turning it
once a day. Then take the Beef out and see that
the fat and lean lie equal: then take some Pepper, Cloves and Mace [5] A good deal of Parsley
and sweet Majoram shred small, mix these ingredients together and strew it over the inside
of the Beef; then role it hard and fillet it close
and sew it up in Cloth and tie it at both ends, in
this Condition put it into a deep pan with the
Pickle and a pint of Water. You may also add a
pint of Claret and must put in an Onion stuck
with Cloves and a pound of Butter. Then cover
the Pan with a coarse past, and bake it all day.
Then take it hot and role it harder, and put it to
stand on one end, and a Plate at the Top and a
weight on it, and let it stand till tis Cold. Then
take it out of the Cloth and keep it dry.

---

8. A piece of meat was collared by being given various
flavors, rolled up tightly, and bound with tape or cloth
before being cooked.

9. Salt peter (potassium nitrate) was commonly used
by eighteenth-century cooks as a food preservative.

χ To Pott Beef like Venison[10]

Cut Eight Pound of Lean Beef out of the But-
tock or any other lean peice into Pound Peices,
take six Ozs. salt Peter, half a pint of Peter
Salt[11] and as much Common salt and rub the
meat well with it and let it lie three or four
days, then put it into a stone jarr and cover it
with some of its own Brine and Pump Water
and bake it, then Pick all the fatt and Skins
from it and pound it very fine in a Marble Mortar; as you pound it pour in melted Butter
enough to make it very moist, like paste. Add
peper and salt to Your tast, and season it high
with Spices. Then press it down in your Pot,
and cover it with Clarified Butter or Mutton
Suet.

---

10. This is one of the recipes taken by Harriott from
her mother's cookbook wherein Eliza had added a
comment: "Extreamly good. (My own way)." Eliza's pride
notwithstanding, this recipe is a reworking, with few
changes, from one in [Hannah Glasse], *The Art of
Cookery, Made Plain and Easy* (London, 1747), p. 253.

11. Niter "in its native State" was called peter salt;
when refined, salt peter. See *Oxford English Dictionary*,
s.v., "petre." This work is cited hereinafter as *OED*.

χ [6] To Ragout a Breast of Veal

Take a large Breast of Veal, more than half roast it, cut it into four peices and have ready as much strong gravy as will cover it. Put it into your stew pan, season it high with Pepper, Cloves, Mace, and Nutmeg, a little Chalot, Lemon Peal, mushrooms, Oysters fried and stew'd; Sweet Breads skin'd and Pull'd in little peices, and when it is done enough fry your largest Oysters with Crispt Bacon and forced Meat Balls and put them in. But for a white ragoe take the same ingredients only boil the Breast of Veal in half Milk and water; with a bunch of sweet herbs, a little Lemon Peel, Mace, and whole Pepper; when it is enough wash it over with the Yolks, and a little Butter and put it into your Stew Pan, just long enough to make it look Yellow and thicken your sauce with the Yolks of Eggs, and a peice of Butter rowl'd up in flow'r with three Spoonfulls of Cream thickned up to-gether.

x ## To Dobe a Rump of Beef[12]

Bone it and lard it with Bacon, Season it with
Sweet herbs, Challots, Pepper, and Salt, Put it
into your Pot (with just water enough to cover
it) with Carrotts, Turnips, Onions, and whole
Pepper, cloves and Mace; let it stew over a slow
fire for three hours till tender, then make a
good Sauce with rich gravey, Morrells, Truffles,
and Mushrooms over it.

x [7] ## To Stew Pidgions[13]

Take the Pidgions and draw them at the Neck,
Wash them and wipe them dry, take a peice of
Veal and chop it with a little Suet, sweet herbs,

---

12. This is a *daube,* from the French *daubière,* a
covered casserole. France has many regional *daubes* in
which the meat is marinated in wine with vegetables and
sometimes, as here, larded. English cooks did not often
use *daubes,* but examples appear in Elizabeth Raffald,
The Experienced English Housekeeper . . . . (London,
1771), pp. 80, 170, and Elizabeth Cleland, *A New and
Easy Method of Cookery* . . . . (Edinburgh, 1770), pp. 29,
49. In America the very accomplished Mary Randolph
had *daubes* in her *The Virginia Housewife: or, Methodical
Cook* (Baltimore, 1836), pp. 33, 66, 152. According to
Karen Hess, this work's recipes may date from the 1790s.
See Hess, *Martha Washington's Booke,* p. 6.

13. In America this dish would have been used for the
carrier pigeons that wintered along the southern coasts
by the millions and were taken at night by torchlight,
beaten from their low roosts. See Hooker, *Food and
Drink,* pp. 54–55.

pepper, salt, Nutmeg, and Crumbs of Bread, then take an Egg and mix it well together and put in the Crops and Bodies, and tie up the Necks and vents very close dredge them and put them in a Frying Pan and fry them Brown and let your Butter be hot and drain them and put them into a Pan with gravy, Morels, Troufles Pepper Salt and Mace and stew them till they are tender then thicken them up with Butter and Flower and a little lemon Peel grated into it and some Juice of Lemon Squeezed into it. You may Put the Livers and Gizzards if you Please and Serve it up.

Beef Collops

Take a Rump of Beef, cut the Collops the length of the rump very thin, beat them very tender, season them with Pepper and Salt, and flower them very well, put some butter into the Stew pan make it very Hott, but not burn it, put the Collops in the Stew Pan when the butter is hot and set them on the stove over a slow fire till they are warm through take them out of the Stew pan and cover them down till you are ready to send them to Table. Make some rich Gravy put some Morrels in it and Season it to your Taste let them simmer in the Gravey about a Quarter of an Hour before you send them to table. Send them up very Hott.

[8] To Dress a Calves head in imitation of Turtle

Take a Calves head with the Skin on scald and clean it like a Pigg. Then Parboil it that the Bones may come easily out. Set by the Water you Parboil it in to make your Soop with. When you have taken the Bones out, cut your Head, Ears, etc. to Pieces. NB The Ears should be cut in long slips the Rest the Size of a Pullets Egg. Take 2 or 3 Pellets stew them tender and cut them in Pieces put all together into the Water you had sett by, stew it down very tender and season it pretty high with Onions and sweet Herbs, Mace, Cloves, Nutmegs, Pepper and Salt to your taste, add to this a Pint and ½ of Madeira Wine, thicken your Soop with the Yolk of an Egg. Your Force Meat for the Balls may be made with a bit of the Head, a bit of Bacon, and seasoned high with Sweet Herbs, add the Yolk of an Egg make it into Balls, fry them, and Put them in your Soop, when you serve it up——

You may Put Sweet Breads, Troufles and Morrels, but if the Head has the Skin on, I think 'tis quite Rich enough without either.

[9]   **To Stew Mushrooms**[14]

Take Your large Mushrooms peel them and put them in a Stew Pan with some salt, whole pepper, and large mace, two or three cloves, let them stew a while over a soft fire then put to them Crumbs of Bread and a little white wine and let them stew a little more, into your dish with a Chalott and stir in a lump of Butter.

14. Mushrooms may not have been commonly eaten in eighteenth-century America. There was certainly no reliable guide to distinguish the edible from the poisonous varieties. Landon Carter and Thomas Jefferson in Virginia both ate mushrooms, and they were advertised for sale in the *South Carolina Gazette.* See Jack P. Greene, ed., *The Diary of Colonel Landon Carter of Sabine Hall, 1752–1778* (Charlottesville, Va., 1965), 2:737, 739; Spruill, *Women's Life,* 276–77. That Harriott offers three recipes for mushrooms is evidence enough that she used them.

To Caveach Mackrel[15]

Cut Your Mackrel into round peices and wipe
them dry divide one into five or six peices, to
six Mackrel you may take one Ounce of Beaten
pepper, three large Nutmegs, a little mace and
a handfull of salt mix your salt and spice and
make two or three holes in each peice and put
the Seasoning into the holes, rub the peices
over with the Spice, and fry them brown in Oil
and let them stand till they are cold, then put
them into your Vinegar cold and cover them
with oil. They will keep well cover'd a great
while and are delicious. The Vinegar should be
boil'd with a little Spice, a good deal of horse
radish and mustard seed, and let stand to be
cold before you put the fish in.

---

15. This recipe comes from Eliza Lucas Pinckney's
cookbook, and she in turn obtained it, directly or
indirectly, from Hannah Glasse's *The Art of Cookery*,
p. 259 of the 1747 edition. The word caveach came from
the Spanish *escabeche*, which in turn has an Arabian
origin. See Hess, *Martha Washington's Booke*, pp. 177–78.
A New England cookbook stated that to caveach fish was
"as practised in the West Indies." *Mrs. Gardiner's
Receipts from 1763*, p. 29. Early English recipes appear
in Raffald, *The Experienced English Housekeeper*,
pp. 350–51.

[10] ## To Stew Crabs

Choose three or four Crabs, pick the Meat clean
out of the body and claws, take care no spungy
part be left among it or any of the Shell, put
this clean meat into a stew pan, with a little
white wine, some pepper and salt, and a little
grated Nutmeg, heat all this, well together, and
then put in some Crums of Bread, the yolks of
two Eggs beat up and one Spoonfull of Vinegar.
Stir all well together, make some toasted Sippets, lay them in a plate and pour in the crabs.
Send it up hott.

Stew'd Ducks

Take a Duck (either wild or tame) split it down
the back, make some Stuffing with Stale bread,
the Liver of the duck, Spice, Parsley, Marjoram,
Onion, Butter, Pepper and Salt, all chop'd up
together, fill the duck with it and sew up the
back, and put it into a Pott with Water enough
to cover it let it stew till the Water is almost
stew'd away then add a little Wine and a lump
of Butter to the little that remains which
makes the gravy and browns the Duck.

Sausages

Take ten pounds of the lean Meat of a Hog,
Eight pounds of hard fat, chop it very fine and
take out all the strings and gristles, then mix
in one oz. Pepper, ¼ oz. Mace ¼ oz. cloves ½ oz.
Nutmeg ½ oz. All spice[16] and ½ oz. salt Peter
dried Sage, Thyme, and Parsley. Mix all well
together with salt to your tast, moisten it with
Water and a little Madeira Wine and put it in
the large Guts

NB: the skins should lay 1 night in Salt.

x [11]   # To pickle Shrimps

Boil your Shrimps in strong salt and Water till
the shells will easily peel off, take them off and
put them to cool while you prepare the following pickle. Take of the liquor the shrimps were
boild in and strong vinegar equal parts (a
quantity fully sufficient to cover the shrimp) to
this put some black pepper, All spice and cloves
coarsely pounded, and boil it till it is strong of
the spice, then strain and set it to cool. Pick
your shrimps and put them in a pot with a
blade or two of mace and a few cloves and pour
the pickle cold over them. Should the weather
be very hot add a little salt.

---

16. The British and the Americans obtained allspice
from the British West Indian islands where it was
indigenous.

x

White Sauce for cold Veal or Lamb sliced thin or chicken

Take half a pint of Milk thicken it with a little Flour a little bit of Butter a blade of Mace and a Little nutmeg grated.

x

Vinegar

Take 10 lb. coarse sugar and 10 Galls. Water, boil them together skiming it well as long as any scum will arise, then put it into tubs and when about half cold put in a thick slice of bread Toasted and well soaked with yeast, let it work in the tubs twenty four hours then put it into a cask iron hoop'd and well painted and fixed in a place where the Sun has full power and so as to have no occasion to move it. cover the bung to keep the dirt out. it will generally be fit to use in about four Months, then draw it off for use, but if not soon enough let it stand a month longer.

[12] To make a Cassorol or rather a rice pye[17]

In the first place you must have a copper Pan well tined. A Tin pan will not do. —Boil 3 pints of rice rather softer than you do rice in Common grease the pan well with Butter and press it (the rice) well into the pan round the sides and bottom and top and put to Bake at the fire turning it round constantly as it will burn. When it is done of a good light brown turn it out on a Dish and cut out in the middle in the middle [*sic*] sufficient to make room for a rich Fill as a Beef or veal or any thing you please.

x [13] Portugal cakes

Take 1 lb. flour, 1 lb. Sugar finely powder'd mix them together and dry them before the fire. Take 1 lb. Butter and beet it till it is soft and add to it six Eggs leaving out 2 of the whites, beet them well together and add to them half of the sugar and flour and beet it all to-gether till the Oven is ready and just before you put it in the oven add the other half of the sugar and flour, a

---

17. This recipe could have had a French origin, or a French West Indian one. For what it is worth a very similar recipe, but using a mold to create a center space for the meat fill, is in *The Picayune Creole Cook Book* (New Orleans, 1916), p. 117.

little Mace and a little rose Water,[18] mix them all together put them into your pans and sprinkle fine sugar over them and bake them in a light oven. Some add ½ pound of Corinths.[19]

Ice for Plumb cake

x

For a pound cake Take 1 lb. of fine loaf sugar beat it and sift it. Take the whites of Eight Eggs, beat them in a dish to a stiff froth then put the sugar into a Mortar and add the Eggs by degrees to it with a little rose Water and the juice of a lemon or a couple of limes, rub it altogether in the mortar till it is very white and smooth then lay it on the cakes with a knife and put them in an oven not hot but warm enough to dry them.

---

18. Rose water was made from fresh rose petals and was used as a flavoring by the English from the sixteenth through the eighteenth centuries. See Wilson, *Food and Drink,* p. 399.

19. Corinths was an alternative name for currants.

x

Pap Pudding

Take 2 spoons full of rice flour (such as for Journey cake) boil it into a Pap with a gill of milk and a gill of Water, when cold put to it 5 Eggs (1 white) ½ Nutmeg a large spoon full of Butter a heaped spoonful of Corinths and sugar to your taste, bake it without crust and for an hour will bake it.

To preserve small green Oranges

Grate the outside rind off with a fine bread grater then boil them for (say ½ an hour) till you can run a straw thro them. put them into cold Water and change it 2 or 3 times a day for a week or till all the bitterness is out. Then take equal weight of sugar and cover the oranges and let them lay all night, then boil them till they are done and look clear.

x [14] **To make Sweetmeat Jelly**

Take two calves feet, half a pound of hartshorn Shavings[20] and an Ounce of Isinglass,[21] put them into five pints of Spring Water, let it boil over a Slow fire till it comes to three pints. Let it stand to be intirely cold, and then take off the fatt from top and bottom. put it into your sauce pan and rest it and add to it a quart of white wine and a Gill of Sack,[22] the whites of ten Eggs well beat, a little lemon Peal and a bit of Cinnamon and sugar to your tast. Set it on the fire and keep it stiring till it has one good boil up, then take it off the fire, thro in a full gill of Lemon juice and putt it into your Jelly Bag which observe to have ready wash'd with a little wine.

Never let the Jelly have more than one boil up and be sure not to put in the Juice till 'tis taken off the fire.

---

20. Deer antlers, "hart's horn," were shaved and used to provide a gelatine.

21. Isinglass was another form of gelatine, made from the bladder of the sturgeon.

22. Sack usually referred to wines from southern Spain and the Canary Islands.

x ## To make Pompion Chips[23]

Shave your Pompion thin with a plain and cut it in slips about the width of your finger, put shreds of Lemon peal among it, wet your sugar with orange Juice and boil it into Syrup. Then put in your chips and lemon Peal and let them boil till done.

x [15] ## To make Almond Cream

Take half a pound of good Jordan Almonds[24] blanch and beat them very fine with Orange Flower Water,[25] take a quart of Cream boil'd, cool'd, and sweetend to your tast put the Almonds into it and when they are mix'd strain it through a peice of Canvas, then stir it over the fire till it thickens, and then pour it in your Glasses.

Irish Butter

Take an Ounce and half of Isinglass, put half a pint of Spring Water, let it simmer till 'tis dissolved, then put in a pint and a quarter of

---

23. Pompion was long used in England and America as the word for pumpkin.

24. Almonds had come to England and its colonies from Spain. Jordan was the Middle English *jardyne* which very likely came from the French *jardin,* garden. See Hess, *Martha Washington's Booke,* p. 328.

25. This was made from orange flowers but was less common than rosewater. See Wilson, *Food and Drink,* p. 356.

Water and a quarter of a pint of Mountain Wine,[26] the Juice of one Lemon and the peal of half a one pared thin, a very little saffron[27] and sugar to your tast, let all boil together a quarter of an hour strain it in a dish through Muslin and cut it out in what form you please.

To make Snow Cream[28]

A quarter of a pound of roasted Apple a quarter of a pound of fine Sugar beaten and sifted, the Juice of two lemons and the whites of six Eggs; Beat these all together in the manner you do Floating Island. put some grated Lemon Peel, orange flower Water, and fine Sugar into half a Pint of Cream, [16] let it stand some time, then strain it into your dish, and put some froth gentle upon it.

---

26. Mountain wine was made of mountain-grown Malaga grapes, though in England, and later in America, it came to be simply a wine made with Malaga raisins. See E. Smith, *The Compleat Housewife* . . . . (London, 1730), p. 221; R. Bradley, *The Country Housewife and Lady's Director* . . . . (London, 1736), p. 66; Richard Briggs, *The English Art of Cookery* . . . . (Dublin, 1798), p. 501.

27. Saffron had colored and flavored sauces in England since the middle ages, and as late as the eighteenth century it was still added to jellies and cakes. See Wilson, *Food and Drink,* p. 294.

28. Snow cream, the froth from beaten egg whites and cream, had been popular in England since Elizabethan times. See ibid., pp. 147, 170.

To Bake Pares[29]

Be sure to bake them in pewter and cover them with Pewter. After they are pared and cut in halves put to them a little red wine, sugar and a little Water and some Cloves, lay them in your dish and bake them in a Soaking Oven,[30] and let them stay till they are of a deep Colour they must be very tender but not Mash'd. When done if the Syrup is not thick enough add a little Sugar to it and boil it up to a proper thickness.

---

29. This is one of the recipes which Harriott had taken from the cookbook of her mother. To it Eliza had added a comment: "My own Tried often and found very good."

30. One meaning of the word soak, during the seventeenth and eighteenth centuries, was to bake thoroughly. See *OED,* s.v., "soak."

Black Caps[31]

Cut your Apples in half. Lay them on a
Mazarine Dish[32] or for want of that on the
Brim of another Dish. Your Apples must not be
Pared lay the cut side upon the Dish, wet the
top of your Apples about an Inch square with
White Wine, and strew Fine Sugar upon the
Wett Place and bake them. take care they dont
Fall too much in the Oven.

---

31. Some early British recipes make clear the name of
this dish. One used rosewater to moisten, with the apples
baked until the skins were somewhat blackened. Cleland,
A New and Easy Method, p. 173. Another baked the
halved apples until they looked "very bright, and very,
very black," and then surrounded them with a thick
cream custard or white wine and sugar. Raffald, *The
Experienced English Housekeeper,* p. 170. A third recipe
had the apples halved and rubbed with egg white, sliced
lemon peel and sugar before being baked, with no
mention of blackened tops. Richard Briggs, *The New Art
of Cookery* . . . . (Philadelphia, 1792), p. 467.

32. A deep pie dish or pan.

Plumb Marmalade

Put the Plumbs in as much Water as will cover them and Scald them soft. Take out the Stones, and blanch the Kernels, put them all together in the Syrup and boil it till it Jellies. Make the Syrup with the Water that Plumbs were Scalded in—about 1 lb. of Sugar to a lb. of Plumbs.——

[17] **Orange Marmalade**

Take Equal weight of Sugar and Oranges. grate off the Yellow outer rind of one half of the Oranges, then cut them all through the Middle and take the Pulp and Juice carefully out of the whole. Pick the seeds from it and throw them into about a quart of water and let them stand till they Jelly. Put your Skins into a large quantity of Water and let them Boil (Supplying with Boiling Water as it boils away) till they are soft and tender, then take out all the inner Skins and Strings and throw them away; then Beat your Skins to a Past, reserving a few of the Yellow Skins to be cut in long, Square, or triangular Pieces, All this being done put the Sugar Juice and Pulp on the Fire and when the Sugar is Melted and begins to Boil add by degrees the Beaten Skins and the Jelly from the Seeds, stirring it constantly till you bruise any

Lumps there may be, let it boil to a proper Consistence observing to throw in the Chips and the greatest Part of the Grateings a little before it is sufficiently Boiled.——

NB The Quart of Water is for the Seeds of about a Dozen pound of Oranges.——

For an Easier and better receipt see page 35.

Almond Cream[33]

Take half a Pound good Jordan Almonds blanch and Beat them very fine with Orange flower water. take a quart of Cream, boil it and when 'tis cold sweeten it to your taste and put the Almonds into it. When they are mix'd strain it thro' a peice of Canvas and stir it over a fire till it thickens. Pour it in Glasses.

x [18] ## Cocoa Nut Puffs

Take a Cocoa Nut and dry it well before the fire, then grate it and add to it a good spoonfull of Butter, sugar to your tast, six Eggs with half the whites and 2 spoonfulls of rose water. Mix them all together and they must be well beat before they are put in the Oven.

---

33. This is almost identical to the recipe on p. 15. Had Harriott forgotten that she had already inserted it?

x

Cheese Cakes

Take a quart of Milk and Turn it with Rennet
or Wine. then turn it into a sieve and let it
drain but do not press it. add to the Curd a
quarter of a pound of Butter, [the yolks of ten
eggs], a quarter of a pound of almonds beat, a
quarter of a pound Currants, half a Nutmeg, a
Glass of sweet wine, a little Orange flower
Water, Citron and Sugar to your tast. —Instead
of turning the Milk with Eggs, 'tis best to turn
it with Rennet or Wine, then add the Eggs and
other ingredients as above.[34]

Ginger Bread

Take three quarts of Flour, two pounds of trea-
cle, half a pound of Sugar, two ozs. of Candied
Orange and Lemon Peel, and one ounce of Ginger and new spices together. mix these altogether as stiff as it can be made and bake it
in an Oven. You must also add a Gill of good
thick Cream, and a spoonful of Fresh Butter.

For a better receipt see page 23.

---

34. Harriott took this recipe from Eliza Lucas
Pinckney's cookbook. In that work Eliza called for
beating the yolks of ten eggs, adding them to the quart
of milk and stirring the mixture over a fire until it
became a curd. Eliza Lucas Pinckney receipt book,
SCHS.

x [19]   # Egg Pyes

Take the Yolks of twenty-four Eggs boil'd hard and half the whites, chop'd with double the quantity of Beef Suet and half a pound of Pippins[35] pared, cored and sliced. Then add to it one pound of Currants wash'd and dry'd, half a pound of sugar, a little salt, some spices beaten fine, the Juice of a Lemon and half a pint of Sack, Candied Orange and Citron cut in Peices of each three Ozs.; Fill the Pastry pans full, the Oven must not be two hott, three quarters of an hour will bake them.

x   # Mackaroons

Blanch a pound of Almonds, and beat them in a Marble Mortar with one pound of Sugar, a little rose Water, and the whites of three Eggs beat to a froth. When it is beat very fine make it Scalding hott drop it upon Wafers and bake it on tin plates. be sure the Oven is not too hott.

---

35. The word pippin could refer either to a seedling apple or to any one of many varieties thought to have superior dessert quality.

Blanc Manger

Take one ounce of Isinglass, pick it fine, put it in a Pint of Milk and let it Simmer 'till 'tis resolved, sweeten it to your tast and you may add half an Ounce of almonds blanch'd and finely beaten, strain it thro' a cloth; stir it till almost cold then put it into the Moulds. When you omit the Almonds put a little orange flow'r or rose water.

[20] ## Orange Puding

Take the rinds of Three Oranges Boild tender and beat very fine, add to it the Juice of two Oranges, a quarter of a pint of Wine with a little spice boil'd in it, six Eggs (half the Whites) well Beat with half a pound of Sugar and half a pound of Butter. Mix all together and bake it very thin.

x ## Yam Puding

Take a pound of Yam boil'd dry, beat it fine in a Mortar with a pound of Butter till it Puffs, take ten Eggs (half the Whites) beat them with a pound sugar, add half a pint of Wine, stew'd with a little spice, the Juice of a Lemon with a little of the rine, and some slices of Citron[36] laid on the Top.

Carrot Puding

Take a large Carrot, boil it Tender then set it by to be cold and grate it through a hair seive very fine, then put in half a pound of melted Butter beaten with Eight Eggs leaving out half the Whites, two or three Spoonfulls of Sack and Orange flower Water, half a pint of good thick cream, a little grated Bread, a Nutmeg and a little salt, sweeten it to your tast, and make it of the thickness of an Orange Pudding.

𝓍
𝓍 [21]   ## Little Pudings

Take one quart of Milk, six Eggs, half a Nutmeg a tea spoon full of Salt, and four table spoonfulls of Flour beat the Eggs, flour etc. well together and pour the milk to them just before you put it in the Oven. Bake them in half pint Bowles and the same baking that does a Custard will be sufficient for them. for sauce melted Butter, a little wine, Sugar and Nutmeg.

---

36. This lemon-like citrus fruit was used both in England and the colonies. Its preserved rind was especially in demand for cakes and puddings.

Mince Pyes

Shred 2 lb. of lean Meat (the inside of the Sir-
lion is best with 3 and ½ lb. of Beef Suet very
small, Season it with One Oz. of Cloves, Mace,
Cinimon and a little Salt, 1 lb. Sugar 8 Oz.
Candied Orange and Cytron together 4 Oz. of
Dates a little lemon peal shred small 3 lb. Currants 1 lb. Rasons stewd and shred the juce of 3
lemons a few Apples Shred and a Pint of Sack.

Apple Pudding

Take eight apples, pare them, core and quarter
them, boil them till they are so tender you may
mash them with a spoon. Sweeten them to your
taste, and add a good large Spoonfull of fresh
Butter, Eight Eggs with half the whites well
beat up and a little beaten Cinnamon. grate in
the rind of a Lemon and the juice of one and
mix it all together and bake it. It is much the
better for some Citron cut in pieces and put in.

[22] To preserve Quinces[37]

Take an equal quantity of Quinces and Sugar,
wash and wipe them very clean, pare them and
put the Skins into a bowle of Water, slice the
quinces very thin and put them into a sauce
Pan with the sugar, strain the Water the Skins
were in and pour over them, there should be
just Water enough to cover the Quinces and
Sugar when you press them gently down with
your hand in the sauce pan. boil it all together
pretty quick till the Syrup thickens a little. If
you chuse to preserve the Quinces whole or in
quarters, you must first boil them in Water till
they are tender, and make the Syrup with the
Water they are boil'd in, then put them into the
Syrup and let them simmer till they are of a
bright red colour, then take them up and if the
Syrup is not quite thick enough boil it up a little and pour over the quinces.

---

37. Quinces were widely grown and used in colonial
America, as they had long been in England. John
Lawson, at the beginning of the eighteenth century,
noted that the Carolina settlers made a "Quince-drink"
that he preferred to their cider and perry. John Lawson,
A New Voyage to Carolina, ed. Hugh Talmage Lefler
(Chapel Hill, 1967), p. 82.

Rusks[38]

Take half a pint of good Leaven or Yeast, half a
pint of warm Milk, five Ounces of Butter, half a
pound of Sugar and five Eggs; beat up the Eggs,
Sugar, and Butter to-gether and mix with half
your flour adding the Leaven and Milk, and let
it stand till 'tis well risen, then mix in the rest
of your flour, knead it well and let it rise again.
Then make them in small Loaves let them rise
a third time and bake them.

This is not so good as the following.

[23] A Better receipt for Rusks than the former

Work well together with your hands 10 Ozs.
Sugar and 10 Ozs. Butter: beat up 10 Eggs with
a pint of Milk, strain it into the butter and
Sugar and add to it half a pint of good Leaven
or Yeast well raised. mix in as much Flour as
will bring it to the consistence of soft Bread, set
it to rise, when it is well risen role it into rusks
with as little flour as possible and when these
begin to rise put fine in your Oven. Make the
Leaven for your rusks in this Manner. Take 4
Eggs, beat them up with a little Brown Sugar,

---

38. Rusks were usually small, sweet, crisp rolls that
were frequently served with afternoon tea during the
eighteenth and early nineteenth centuries.

add to it about half a pint of Milk and a little Flour and two spoonfulls of good bread Leaven, mix it all well to-gether and put it by the fire and let it stand all night.——

A Very good Puding—
Colossus Puding.

One Pound of Sugar, ½ pound of Butter, 8 Eggs half the Whites, a whole Nutmeg, one gill of Juice and some Orange or Lemon Peel grated into it, beat it well to-gether and bake it as you do an Orange Puding.

Very good Ginger Bread

Take one quart Molasses, 3 quarts Flour, a large spoonfull of Butter, 2 Ozs. Ginger and 2 Ozs. China Orange Peel[39] dried and finely powder'd. 4 Eggs whites and Yolks—half a pound of Sugar and some Allspice. Mix all these ingredients well together with 2 or 3 spoonfulls of good yeast. work it up well and role it out and bake it on tin, first Buttering the sheets. You may add 2 ozs. Carraway seed finely powder'd.

---

39. In the seventeenth century the English obtained from Portugal, where it had recently come from China, an orange with a sweet and edible rind and reputedly the best kind to preserve whole. See Wilson, *Food and Drink,* pp. 344–45.

x [24]   # Shrewsbury Cakes[40]

Take one pound of Flour, ½ pound of Butter, ¾ of a pound Sugar 4 Eggs whites and Yolks, a good deal of Mace, a little Nutmeg and 2 spoonfulls of rose water; beat it up well and drop it on Tin Sheets (a pap spoonfull in a drop) grate a little fine sugar over them and bake them in a light Oven. Memorandum I find puting only a pound of Flour makes them rather too thin, therefore 'tis best to add a little more.

x   # German Puffs[41]

Take a quart of Flour and pour about ½ pint of Boiling Water to it, stir it over the fire 'till 'tis quite stiff, then put it into a Marble Mortar and break into it by degrees a dozen Eggs with half the whites; pound it very well and drop it into boiling Lard and let them Fry till they are of a light Brown.

---

40. These flat, round biscuit-like cakes had grown in favor in England in the seventeenth century. See ibid., pp. 268–69.

41. An English recipe for German Puffs is in Elizabeth Raffald, *The Experienced English Housekeeper* (London, [1769]). A South Carolina cookbook of *ca.* 1840 has a recipe for "Yorkshire German Puffs." Anonymous cookbook in the Gibbes-Gilchrist Collection, SCHS.

Potatoe Puding made with Potatoe Powder[42]

Take two large spoonfulls of the Powder, and pour to it by degrees a pint of Milk or a pint of Water, but be very certain it boils before you mix it, then add Eggs, Butter etc. as in a Common Potatoe Pudding and bake it.

x [25]   ## To make Biscuit[43]

Take a quart of Milk make it just hot enough to melt the Butter and then put into it one good spoonfulls of Butter, pour this into as much flour as will knead up into a very stiff dough about 5 pints. Knead it well for an hour and when 'tis quite light role it out (but not too thin) and cut the biscuits out with a Cup. It should be baked in a pretty hot oven

---

42. The white, or Virginia potatoes as they were called, remained a specialty food in England through most of the seventeenth century, baked in pies or as a garnish to beef or fowls. During the eighteenth century their use increased. Wilson, *Food and Drink,* pp. 217–18. For sixteenth- and seventeenth-century uses in England see Hess, *Martha Washington's Booke,* pp. 85–87, 275. For American uses of the white potato, where it did not become common until the mid-eighteenth century, see Hooker, *Food and Drink,* pp. 30, 49–50, 76, 118.

43. This is a very early American recipe for what came to be called beaten biscuit. It was later common practice to beat the dough with an axe or club rather than, as here, kneading it.

Bops[44]

x

Take about a pound of Flour and rub into it a
pap spoonfull of Butter then add as much Milk
as will make it into a very thick Batter then
put it into a marble Mortar and beat it till 'tis
quite light drop it upon tin Sheets (about a
large spoonfull in a drop) and bake them. They
are to be split and butter'd.
N. B. the Butter should be rub'd in the flour till
you cant feel the Butter.

Ratifia Pudding[45]

x

Blanch in boiling water half a pint of peach kernels (if they are too bitter lay them in cold
water all night), beat them with a little rose
water, sweeten them to your tast and add ¼
lb. Butter the yolks of 4 Eggs and a little
Mace. bake them thin. It will answer as well to
make this pudding with Almonds adding about
[*left blank*] Peach Kernels without lay-
ing them in Water.

---

44. This is a misspelling for baps which was, and is, a
small breakfast roll of Scotland. See Elizabeth David,
English Bread and Yeast Cookery (New York, 1980), 320–
23.

45. An obsolete spelling of ratafia, a liquor or cordial
flavored with certain fruits or their kernels.

Strawberry Jelly

Take 6 quarts of Strawberries and 1 quart of Water just boil them up sufficiently to extract the juice, then strain them and to every quart of juice put 1 and ½ lb. of sugar and boil it very quick till it Jellies observing to skim it well.

Catherine

[26]   **Mushroom Catchup
and Powder**[46]

Gather your Mushrooms early in the Morning,
wipe them very clean with a Woolen cloth, then
mash them with the hand, strew on them a
handful of salt, let them lie all night, then put
them on the fire ten minutes, keeping them
constantly stiring, then squeeze them through
a Canvas, and let them settle. Pour it off from
the sediment then put it on the fire and clarify
it with the whites of 2 Eggs. Then put in it
whole Pepper, Cloves, Mace, Ginger, Allspice
and Salt. It must be high season'd. Boil one
part of it away, when cold bottle it puting in the
Spices.

Take 4 lb. Mushrooms that have been squeez'd;
and dry them with a little spice in the Sun or
Oven, and Powder them for Made Dishes.[47]

---

46. For long the Americans, like the English, knew
catchups of mushrooms, anchovies, oysters, or walnuts.
Not until the 1820s, in America, would tomato catchup
begin its rapid rise. See Hooker, *Food and Drink*, p. 118.
A New England cookbook of 1763 gave five recipes for
mushroom catchup and 2 for walnut catchup. *Mrs.
Gardiner's Receipts from 1763*, pp. 66–70.

47. The expression "made dish" has long existed in
England and was used in America into the twentieth
century. It referred to a more elaborate method of
cookery than plain broiling or roasting, or to a
combination of processes, such as making a ragout by

Queen Sauce

Half a pint of good old Walnut Pickle, half a
pint Mushroom Catchup, six Anchovies
minced, six cloves of Garlick, a teaspoonfull
Cayan Pepper Capsicum Persicum:[48] Put all
these ingredients into a Bottle, shake it every
day for a Week then use it.——

Walnut Catchup

Take 50 Walnuts and bruise them well in a
stone Mortar, put in three Pints of the best Vinegar, and stir them every Day for 9 or 10 Day's
together, then strain them through a Muslin,
and boil them a quarter Hour with Mace, whole
Pepper and Nutmeg.

---

half roasting and finishing in a stewpan. See Hooker,
Food and Drink, pp. 77–78, 237. Hannah Glasse gave
rules for made dishes: utensils must be very clean, white
sauces were to be a little tart, and seasonings would
employ such ingredients as truffles, cockscombs,
mushrooms, morels, artichoke bottoms, and asparagus
tips. Mrs. Hannah Glasse, *The Art of Cookery Made
Plain and Easy* (Alexandria, 1805), p. 94. There was a
tendency to identify made dishes with French dishes.

48. This smallest of the American Capsicums was
powdered to make cayenne pepper.

[27] Ats Jaar, or Pucholilla[49]

Take Ginger one Pound, let it lie in Salt and Water one Night, then scrape it and cut it in thin slices, and put it in a Bottle with dry Salt and let it stand till the Rest of the Ingredients are ready. Take one Pound of Garlick divide it in Cloves and Past it. Take small Sticks of about two or three Inches long, and Run them through the Cloves of Garlick. Salt them for three Day's, then wash them, and salt them again and let them stand three Day's longer then salt them and Put them in the Sun to Dry. Take Cabbages cut them in Quarters and Salt them for three Day's then press the Water out of them, and put them in the Sun to Dry.[50] Take

---

49. The origin or meaning of the words Ats Jaar (Ats Jarr in the table of contents) have not been discovered by this editor. Sarah Rutledge, repeating this recipe in *The Carolina Housewife,* p. 179, labeled it simply Atzjar. As for Pucholilla, this was simply one of the innumerable variations of piccalilli. For English recipes similar to Harriott's see that for "Indian Pickle, or Picca Lillo" in Briggs, *The English Art of Cookery,* p. 476; "Indian Pickle, or Peccadillo" in *The London Complete Art of Cookery* (London, 1797), p. 173; and for "Paco lilla, or Indian Pickle" in Hannah Glasse, *The Art of Cookery Made Plain and Easy,* pp. 284–85. However named, the recipe was apparently successful enough to persist. It appeared as "Atx Jar Pickle" in Mrs. B. C. Howard, *Fifty Years in a Maryland Kitchen* (Baltimore, 1873), pp. 279–80.

50. Beginning here Harriott had inserted the following passage, but had at some later time crossed it out: "In

long Pepper[51] Salt it and dry it in the Sun take ½ a pint of Mustard Seed, Wash it very Clean, and lay it to Dry, When it is very Dry bruise half of it in a Mortar take an Ounce of Termarick[52] bruised very Fine, put all these Ingredients into a Stone Jar, and put one Quart of the strongest Vinegar to 3 Qts. of small. Fill the Jar 3 Quarters full, and supply it as often as you see Occasion. After the same Manner you may do Cucumbers, Mellons, Plumbs, apples, Carrots, or any thing of that sort. They are to be put all together, and you need never empty the Jar, but as the Season comes in dry the things and put them in, and fill them up in Vinegar. Be Carefull, no Rain or Damp comes to them for that will make them Rott.

---

the same Manner you must do Collyflower, Cellery, and Radishes only scraping the Radishes and leaving the young Tops on, French Beans, and Asparagus must be salted but two Days, and give them a boil up in Salt and Water, and Dry them in the Sun as you do the others."

51. Long pepper was a popular name for cayenne pepper.

52. The use of turmeric had grown during the eighteenth century among those in England and America who wished to make curry "the Indian way." See Wilson, *Food and Drink*, p. 295.

[28] **To Mango Muskmellons or Cucumbers**[53]

Take them before they are half grown, cut a peice out of them and scrape out the inside, then put them into strong Pickle with a peice of Allum the bigness of a Nutmeg in a Copper Kettle; set them on a slow fire, keep them scalding hott constantly till Night, and then take them off if green, if not let them stand on till next Morning or till they are Green: let them stand till they are cold and then fill them with Horseradish scraped, Mustard seed, Garlick and a little sliced Ginger. Then put on the Peices you first cut off, and tie it round with a coarse Thread and lay them in a Jar and pour boiling Vinegar over them. Stop the Jar close and when they begin to Mother pour fresh Vinegar over them.

Memorandum I would not recommend this receipt as 'tis done in Copper; The receipt page 30 I have found answers much better. H.H.

---

53. During the second half of the seventeenth century pickled mangoes reached England from Asia and they were imitated by pickling cucumbers or melons and even onions and peaches. Ibid.

To Keep Tomatoos for Winter use[54]

Take ripe Tomatas, peel them, and cut them in four and put them into a stew pan, strew over them a great quantity of Pepper and Salt; cover it up close and let it stand an Hour, then put it on the fire and let it stew quick till the liquor is intirely boild away; then take them up and put into pint Potts, and when cold pour melted butter over them about an inch thick. They comonly take a whole day to stew. Each pot will make two Soups.

N. B. if you do them before the month of October they will not keep.

---

54. This could well be the earliest reference to tomatoes in any American cookbook. For the various reasons given in the Introduction this is among the recipes that were almost certainly placed by Harriott in the book in 1770.

The tomato, native to tropical America, had been carried to Europe by Spanish explorers and had spread through that continent, becoming popular in both Italy and France by the eighteenth century. Though known to Jefferson and other Virginia gardeners by the late eighteenth century, it would not become widely known in America until the early nineteenth century. See Hooker, *Food and Drink,* pp. 51, 118–19.

[29] **Rennet**[55]

After having wash'd the Bag slightly and salted it, let it lie in the Pickle a day or two, then put a small peice of the Bag into a Tea Cup of warm Water for half an hour, which Water put into two quarts of Milk; when 'tis turn'd add to the Whey half a dozen Cloves two or three Blades of Mace, a handfull of fine Salt and a few Sago Leaves. Boil it a quarter of an hour, let it stand till cold and put the Bag into it for three or four days, then strain the Rennet and Bottle for use. It must be kept very cool and close stop'd. A Large Spoonfull will turn a Gallon of Milk which must be warm from the Cow.

To Pickle Hams, Tongues or Dutch Beef

Take a Gallon of Water and make a brine with half bay salt[56] and half common salt strong enough to bear an Egg add to it one pound of

---

55. Rennet, the digestive juice from the stomach bag of calves and several other mammals, was widely used to turn milk and to make cheese.

56. Bay Salt came from sun-evaporated waters of the French Atlantic coast and the beaches of northern Spain and Portugal. Though dark, coarse, and full of impurities, it was thought best for preserving since it penetrated flesh more thoroughly and made a better cure than other salts. See Wilson, *Food and Drink,* pp. 39–40.

coarse Sugar, a quarter of a pound of salt Peter and two Ozs. Salt Prunella[57] boil all these together and skim it clean. Then, take it off the fire and when 'tis cold put in your meat and let it lie in well cover'd with the Pickle. Hams should be in a month or five Weeks, Beef and Tongues a week less. then take them out and smoke them.

N.B. I prefer Pococks Pickle to this, for Bacon, Beef, Pikled Pork etc.

---

57. Sal-prunella was a preparation of fused niter most commonly used for throat disorders. See *OED*, s.v., "prunella."

x [30] **To Mango Muskmellons and Cucumbers and to pickle French Beans, Girkins etc.**

Take them when they are about one third grown, cut a piece out of the side and scrape out the inside. Then make a brine of salt and Water boiling hot and pour over them; cover the Jar close to keep in all the Steam, you must continue to heat the brine and pour over them every day for 8 or 10 days or till they are quite green, it is best to make fresh brine every three or four days. When they are sufficiently green fill them with horseradish scraped, Mustard seed, Garlick or Eschalots, and a little sliced ginger, tie on the pieces you first cut of, put them in your Jar and pour boiling Vinegar over them.

Memorandum They will at first turn yellow, but continuing the hot brine as above directed they will become green again. H.H.

N. B. You may green oranges for preserving in the same way, then boil them in fresh water (shifting the water) till they are tender, then boil them in a syrup which has been made with 1½ lb. Sugar to a pound of oranges. [*The following was added at some later date in the left hand margin.*] I find it is best to pour the syrup boiling hot over the Oranges in the proportion of ½ to 1 lb. Oranges and not boil the Oranges in the Syrup as that often makes them hard. They should stand some months before they are sufficiently impregnated with the syrup and then I think they are equal to any that are boiled in two or three minutes.

To make good Yeast

Thicken two quarts of Water with about a pint of Wheat Flour, boil it quickly for half an hour and when almost cold stir into it half a pound of sugar and ½ pint Yeast, put it into a Jar and place it before the fire so that it may by a moderate heat ferment, when it appears quite light 'tis sufficiently fermented then put it into a cool place tied close down. We use about a gill of this yeast for a quart of Flour or oven Loaf. Memorandum I rather prefer the yeast mention'd in the next page.

[31]   **Pocock's Pickle**

Take 4 gallons of Water to which add 6 lb. of
Bay or Corning Salt 1 and ½ Muscovade
Sugar[58] and 2 Ozs. salt peter. put it into a pot
or kettle and be carefull to take all the scum off
as it rises. when no more scum rises take the
liquor off and let it stand to be cold. In hot
weather it will be necessary to boil up the
pickle now and then, skiming off all that rises
and throwing in during the boiling 2 Oz. sugar
and ½ lb. comon salt.

1½ lb. salt

For 1 Gallon ½ Oz. salt peter

6 oz. sugar

Soap

First make your Lie strong enough to bear an
Egg, and to every gallon of this strong lie add
[*illegible*] lb. of Tallow or Grease, let the fire be
under it till the grease is melted, then draw the
fire intirely away, stir it well, and in a few
hours you will perceive it to be thick and like
glue, then add salt to part it; skim off the Soap
and throw away the salt Lie, and put the half
done soap back again in the pot (without wait-

---

58. This was simply raw or unrefined sugar.

ing for it to be cold) with more fresh lie, boil it for about an hour, grain it as before, skim off your soap and put it in a box to cool.

Yeast

Take 5 common sized Irish potatoes and boil them in about 4 quarts of Water till they are soft enough to mash. Then add a handful of hops and let it boil up, then take it off the fire let it cool a little and strain it, and put a large spoon-ful of Brown sugar in it. bottle it and keep it warm till it works then put it in a cool place but don't cork it—when you put in the sugar you should always keep a little to begin with. When this yeast is good one pint is sufficient for 2 loaves of Bread.

[32] ## Ratifia

Six hundred peach Kernels sliced to one Gallon Brandy: One Quart of sweet Wine, one Quart Orange flower water 1 pound and ¼ Sugar, infuse all these ingredients in the Sun for Six Weeks, shaking the Jug every Day.—then Filter it for Use.——

Orange Flower Ratifia

One lb. of Orange flowers fresh plucked, One Oz. Cinnamon pounded two Ozs. Peach Kernels. one lb. Sugar, and one quart of boiled Water, cold, put all these ingredients into a Gallon of French-Brandy in a Jug to Ferment for a Month, taking Care to Shake it once or twice a Day.

To make Spruce Beer[59]

Take about half a pound of Spruce or Common Pine Tops, half a pound of China root,[60] half a pound of Sassafrass[61] and one quart of Indian Corn. Put all these ingredients into Seven Gallons of Water and let it boil away to five Gallons or till the Corn begins to Crack open. Take it off the fire and let it stand till 'tis cold, then put it into a Cask with about a pint of Yeast or grounds of Beer and three pints of Molasses, and when it begins to work bottle it. NB: The bottles must be well cork'd.

---

59. This was very popular throughout the colonies, and during the War of Independence it was a common issue to American soldiers. See Hooker, *Food and Drink*, pp. 82–83.

60. This is a shrubby climbing plant akin to sarsaparilla. See *OED*, s.v., "China root."

61. The dried bark of the American sassafras tree was often used to make tea or to flavor.

[33] The Duke of Norfolk Punch[62]

Boil twelve Gallons of Water, as soon as it Boils put in twelve pounds of loaf Sugar and the Whites of thirty Eggs. Let them boil a quarter of an hour, and when cold strain it very clean through a coarse cloth into a rum Cask; then put in five quarts and an half of Orange juice, and three quarts and an half of Lemon juice straind. Peel thirty Oranges and thirty Lemons very thin, steep the Peel in a Gallon of rum four days, strain the rum off into the Cask adding four gallons more of rum. It will be fit to bottle in two Months. Care must be taken not to shake the cask when drawing off.

It may be weaken'd with Water as you use it to the Palate.

---

62. Punch was immensely popular among the American upper classes during the seventeenth and eighteenth centuries. It was made by combining wine, brandy, or rum with citrus fruit juices and water. Great quantities of orange, lemon, and lime juices were imported into the colonies to supply makers of punch. See Hooker, *Food and Drink,* pp. 38, 88–89.

Shrub[63]

To every Gallon of Rum put one Quart of Juice,
and two pounds of best double refined Sugar.
Shake the Shrub every day for two Months, and
let it settle once more, then draw it off for
use.—The Vessel should be kept close cork'd
during the whole process. and to every hundred
of Oranges put twenty-five Lemons. To make
your Shrub fine all the Materials should be of
the best.

Mr. E. Nonfueillonson

[*On the margin of the above recipe Harriott
wrote:*] I think the following receipt better To 1
Gall. old rum 5 pints Juice and 3½ lb. Sugar.

Cherry Brandy

Fill your Cask or Jug full of cherries and then
pour in as much Brandy as it will hold, when it
has stood a sufficient time (about 2 or 3
Months) draw it off. Take ½ an Oz. of Cinnamon or All Spice, put it into 2 quarts of
Water and let it simmer gently away to one
quart; disolve in this quart one pound of loaf
sugar and add this water to each gallon of
cherry Brandy.

---

63. Shrub was of middle eastern origin. It had become
popular in England in the early eighteenth century when
it was made with brandy, lemon juice and peel, sugar
and white wine. A rum-shrub became popular later. See
Wilson, *Food and Drink,* p. 401.

[34] **Plumb Pudding**

Take a pound of suet shred very small, a pound
of raisins stoned (or Corinths) 6 spoonfulls of
Flour, 4 spoon fulls of Sugar, 5 Eggs leaving out
2 Whites, a little salt, and ½ Nutmeg grated,
mix all well together, tie it up close and boil it
at least 4 hours.

x **Ratifia Drops**

Take ½ lb. bitter Almonds, blanch and beat
them very fine with an equal Weight of loaf
sugar, make it into a pretty stiff paste with the
whites of 3 Eggs well frothed; roll them about
the size of a nutmeg, make a dent in the middle, lay them on paper and bake them in a slow
oven.

Mince Pies

Mrs. Joseph Wragg

Take 2 Neats[64] Tongues and corn them for 24 hours, then parboil them and cut away the roots and peel them thin, then chop them up small and add to them, double the weight (of them) of Beef Suet minced fine, as many corinths as the tongues weigh; and as much citron, candied orange Peel and raisins together as the tongues, so that the fruit altogether will be equal to the suet; add also 2 ounces of spice (vizt 2 nutmegs, mace, cloves and cinnamon), half a pound of loaf sugar and the yellow rind of 2 Lemons or Oranges grated, dry all the fruit before the fire that the ingredients may not be put together too moist, mix all well together and put them down close in a wooden vessel and it will keep all the winter; when you make them up add 2 or 3 pippins cut small, a gill of White wine, 3 spoonfulls of orange juice and 2 spoonfulls of Brandy and a little rose water and make this liquor pretty sweet.——

NB. our Tongues common weigh about 1 lb each, so that this quantity contains

of Meat	2 lb	of citron, orange	
Suet	4	peel and raisins	2 lb
Corinths	2	spices	2 ozs.
		sugar	½ lb.

---

64. The word neat, now obsolete, refers to common domestic cattle.

x [35] # Raspberry Jam

Take an equal quantity of raspberries and sugar and put the sugar into your pan with as much water as will disolve it (2 lb. of sugar will require near a pint of water) then put it on the fire let it boil and skim it clean. Mash your raspberries and put them into the syrup and let them boil quick till it jellies, about a quarter of an hour upon good coals is sufficient.

x # Raspberry Vinegar

Take 6 lb. Raspberries, 2 lb. red wine vinegar and 10 lb. Sugar. chuse your raspberries sufficiently ripe but not over ripe, put them into your preserving pan with the vinegar and sugar broke; put it on the fire, let it boil up several times and keep it stiring with a wooden stick, and when it is done to the consistence of a ["syrup" *canceled and an illegible word interlined*] run it thro' a flannel bag.

x Quince Marmalade and preserved Quinces

Put the Quinces into cold Water and boil them till the Skin cracks open, have ready a syrup made with an equal weight of sugar by puting as many whites of eggs as will moisten the sugar and adding as much later as will make it into thick syrup. Then peel the quinces which you will do very easily with your fingers, scrape them down from the core with a spoon and put them into the cold syrup keep it constantly stiring with a wooden stick and let it boil gently till you can see the bottom of the pan, then put it into your pott which should be shallow. [*added in the margin:*] To preserve Quinces whole or in quarters peel them and boil them till they are tender then put them into your syrup and boil them quick till they are of a pink color and sufficiently impregnated with the syrup then take them out and put them in your pots and boil up the syrup till it is thick enough and pour it over them.

x Orange Marmalade

Take 6 lb. of Oranges and one pound more than the same quantity of sugar which must be disolved in a quart of water. grate off the outer yellow rind of half the Oranges then boil the

oranges whole in 3 waters till they are tender
enough to run a straw in them (observing to
boil them in a vessel that covers close enough to
keep in the steam) then cut them thro' the middle and with a long spoon take out the pulp and
inner skins and rub them through a sieve,
while that is doing cut the rind into thin chips
put the sugar and water on the fire and when
you have scum it clear put in the chips and pulp
and boil it all together. it will take near an
hour to boil.

Miss Oliphant

x [36] ## Water Cake

Put ¾ lb. of loaf sugar in a gill of Water, let the
sugar and Water stand on the fire till it is just
hot enough to bear your finger in it, then put
into it 7 Eggs leaving out 2 whites (the Eggs
should be first beat in a dish) when they are
then mix'd wisk them together a full hour, and
when the Oven is ready sift in half a pound of
Flour and stir it up with a wooden spoon but
must not beat it after the flour is in. put it into
a pan cover'd with writing paper (not butter'd).
It must have a quick oven and one hour will
bake it.

x

Thin Naples Biscuits[65]

Take 1 lb. Sugar and 12 Eggs whites and yolks, beat the Whites seperately and as the froth rises throw it in, just before you put it in the oven add ½ lb. Flour, beat it very well to-gether, and put in either a little rose Water, a few peach kernels or Orange Peel, but the principal thing to be observed is to bake it extremely thin, you may bake it on paper or tin sheets.

Wigs[66]

Take 2 lb. Flour, ¼ lb. Butter and ¼ lb. Sugar a little Yeast 2 Eggs and as much Milk as will make it in Paste, mix it all together and work them well and set them by the fire to rise. When well risen then mix it again and make it into shapes, let it rise again then glaze them

---

65. Naples biscuits were similar to ladyfingers and by the eighteenth century were commonly the same. See Hess, *Martha Washington's Booke,* p. 155.

66. Wigs were small cakes, sweetened and normally lightly spiced. The recipe above is unusual in having no spices. For long made as a Lenten specialty, wigs had been known in England as far back as the fifteenth century. By the eighteenth century they were made, in varying degrees of richness, for all classes in England. See Wilson, *Food and Drink,* p. 266; David, *English Bread and Yeast Cookery,* pp. 484–87. Two recipes are given in Cleland, *A New and Easy Method of Cookery,* pp. 155–56, and three in Glasse, *The Art of Cookery,* pp. 169, 170, 258.

the cream free from rankness; a quantity of cream though ever so judiciously taken off the milk, will when suffer'd to stand [38] some time, let fall a greater [*one word illegible*] quantity of milk. It has been discover'd that this milk (or dregs) of the cream which subsides at the bottom of the vessel, becomes rancid much sooner than the cream itself and that being suffer'd to remain at the bottom of the vessel it presently communicates its rancidity to the cream, and if it mixes again with the cream in the churn the butter takes that marbled appearance which we too frequently perceive. Therefore these dregs should never be suffer'd to remain any time under the cream. there are two means of preventing it one by repeatedly stiring them together to prevent them from subsiding, (a good dairy woman stirs her cream in ev'ry time she goes into the dairy) the other is by pouring off the cream into a fresh vessel and leaving the dregs behind. When ever a quantity has subsided and the cream should be shifted every morning and evening into a fresh, clean, well scalded jar or other vessel; Puting a quart of boiling water into each pail of Milk before it is set will take off the rankness of cream produced by turnips. The principal art in churning lies in keeping the cream of a due degree of warmth in the churn and in giving it a regular agitation. If Butter comes too quickly, it is soft and frothy and soon turns rancid, [39]

If too slowly it loses its flavor and texture. from one to two hours is a proper length of time in churning. If the cream be frothy in the Churn open its mouth for a few minutes to let in the air and give the froth time to dissipate. If the Butter come in small particles which are slow in uniting, strain off part of the Butter milk and it will generally sooner gather: when you take it out of the churn spread it thin in a shallow tray and work it well with clean cold water to get out the Butter milk, salt it, let the salt be work'd in, so wash it, and beat it till the water comes off unsullied. but before the dairy woman begins to take the Butter out of the churn she must first scald and then plunge immediately into cold water every Vessel and thing which is to be used about it, in summer when the butter is very soft it is sometimes necessary to rub them after scalding with salt which assists the wood in retaining the moisture and then plunge them into cold water, but there is a finishing operation which gives not only firmness and a wax like texture to the Butter, but it [*one word illegible*] entirely the buttermilk and the water in which it has been wash'd: take a cheese cloth or strainer and being wash'd as above in hot and then dip'd in cold water it must be wrung as dry as possible and the lump of butter must be beaten with the cloth, as the pat of Butter becomes flat role it up [40] with the cloth and again beat it flat and work it well with the cloth, and as the cloth fills with moisture it must be rewash'd and wrung, each pound of Butter requires in cool weather 4 or 5 minutes. It is of essential service in warm weather as the coolness of the cloth assists in giving firmness to the Butter.—The shape of a Butter Jar should be that of a Cone, namely wider at Bottom than at top, the top should be sufficiently wide to admit its being fill'd conveniently but not wider, this form prevents the butter from rising in the Jar and prevents the air from insinuating itself between the Jar and the Butter. The Method of puting it down is this, the Butter having lain in pound lumps 24 hours, the dairy Woman takes two or three of the lumps, joins them together, and kneads them in the manner in which paste is kneaded, this brings out a considerable quantity of watery brine which being pour'd out of the tray the Butter is beaten with a cloth as before, and the Jar being previously boil'd and having stood [41] to be perfectly cool and dry the Butter is thrown into it and kneaded down as close and firm as possible with the knuckles and the cloth alternately, being careful not to leave any hollow cell or vacuity for the air to lodge in more particularly round the outsides between the Butter and the Jar, and for this purpose the fingers should be repeatedly drawn round the sides of the jar, pressing the Butter hard, and thoroly uniteing intimately the jar and the

Butter; it is fortunate when the Jar can be fill'd
at one churning, but when this canot be done
conveniently, the top must be left level, and
when the next churning is added, the surface is
raised into inequalities and the two churnings
united into one Mass.—the Jar being fill'd with
Butter to within two or three inches of the top
it must be fill'd up with brine made by boiling
salt and water in the proportion of a handful to
a pint ten minutes or a quarter of an hour,
straining it and when perfectly cool putting it
upon the Butter about 1½ or two inches thick.
If a wooden Bung be put upon this and a bladder tied over that, butter thus preserved will
remain perfectly sweet almost any length of
time provided the jars are placed in a *dry* and
cool situation—see page 46.

x [42]   **Fish Sauce**

Take 1 lb. Anchovies, 1 pint port wine, ½ pint
strong Vinegar an Onion, a handful of Thyme,
2 or 3 cloves, a few blades of mace, a little allspice and whole pepper, a large lemon sliced
with the skin on, cover it close to keep in all the
steam and stew it gently till the Anchovies
bones are all dissolved then strain it and bottle
it for use. You may mix it with melted butter to
bring to Table. it is best to let it stand some
weeks before it is used.

Portugal Cakes[67]

x

Take 1 lb. Flour well dried and 1 lb. Sugar, mix them well together, work a pound of Butter till it is soft as pap then by degrees strew in half the flour and sugar working it well all the time, then add the yolks of six Eggs and but 2 whites, and while the oven is [*one word illegible*] work in the rest of the flour and sugar, 4 spoonfulls of rose water and a little fine mace, butter the pans thin, and fill them but half full pressing them in the pans that they may spread, dust a little sugar over them and ¼ of an hour will bake them.

Very light little cakes
or Citron Biscuits

x

Take 1 lb. loaf sugar pounded fine grate in the rind of one Lemon and the juice of one, mix it together, then take the white of one Egg which has been well beaten to a froth, rub them all together in the Mortar till it is quite white then sugar your roling pin and role it out sprinkling a little sugar on the Table, cut it in slips and bake on paper be careful the oven is not too hot.

---

67. This recipe is certainly the same as that on p. 13, but so changed in wording as to suggest that Harriott may have received it from the same person on two different occasions, perhaps many years apart.

x [43]   **Jumbles**[68]

Take 4 Eggs leaving out 2 of the whites, half pound Butter, 1 lb. Sugar beat them up together as for pound cake, then thicken it with flour till it comes like thin paste which will take about 2 lb. of flour which must be well dried. Sprinkle in some carraway seeds, a glass of Brandy, and a tea cup of rose water; role them out with the hand and make them into small circles, then dip them into pounded sugar and put them on tin sheets and bake them.

---

68. The jumbal, as it had long been spelled in England, was a small cake, its name derived from the gemmel, or twin finger-ring, fashioned as interlaced rings, knots, or other similar shapes. See Wilson, *Food and Drink,* p. 269, and Hess, *Martha Washington's Booke,* p. 349. A contemporary American recipe for "Fruit Jumbals," in which fruit pulp is boiled, mixed with sugar, and dried before making into knots, is in "The Ashfield Recipe Book," in New Jersey Historical Society, *Pleasures of Colonial Cooking* (Orange, N.J., 1982), p. 144.

To preserve peaches

Take the peaches full grown and ripe but not soft, weigh them and to every pound of peaches take ½ lb. sugar. pare the peaches very thin and put them in a jar sprinkling the sugar between every layer of Peaches, let them lay 12 hours in which time the juice will be drawn, then put them in some preserving pan and boil them till transparent then put them in bottles or small jars puting in 2 or 3 glasses of Brandy to each while warm. N.B. when you do a good many peaches ½ lb. sugar to a pound peaches is sufficient, but if only 2 or 3 lb. are done it will require ¾ lb. to each pound.   Very good

Another Way

Take your peaches wash them and rub them well to get off the down, then to every pound of peaches take ¾ lb. of Sugar and put it into your pan with just Water enough to damp it, put it on the fire and when it is melted skim it well and drop your peaches in but not so many as to crowd it, you must watch them well and as soon as the peaches begin to crack take them out and put them in a dish and put in more peaches and do them in the same way till all the peaches are done then boil up your syrup thick enough and to every pint of syrup put a pint of Brandy and pour over the peaches. Mrs. Rowe.

[44] Forsyth's Directions for making a Composition for curing diseases, defects, and Injuries in all kinds of fruit and forest trees, and the method of preparing the Trees, and laying on the composition, by William Forsyth. of Kensington.——

Take one Bushel of fresh Cow dung, half a bushel of lime rubbish of old buildings (that from the cielings of rooms is preferable) half a bushel of wood ashes, and a sixteenth part of a bushel of pit or river sand: the three last articles are to be sifted fine before they are mixed, then work them well together with a spade, and afterwards with a wooden beater, until the stuff is very smooth, like the fine plaister used for the cielings. —The composition being thus made, care must be taken to prepare the tree properly for its application, by cutting away all the dead, decayed, and injured parts till you come to the fresh, sound wood, leaving the surface of the wood very smooth, and rounding off the edges of the bark with a draw-knife, or other instrument perfectly smooth, which must be particular attended to; then lay on the plaister, about one eighth of an Inch thick, all over the part where the wood or bark has been so cut away finishing off the edges as thin as possible; then take a quantity of dry powder of wood ashes, mixed with a sixth part of the same quantity of the ashes of burnt bones; put it into a tin box, with holes in the top, and shake the powder on the surface of the plaister, till the whole is covered over with it, letting it remain for half an hour, to absorb the moisture, then apply more powder, rubbing it on gently with the hand, and repeating the application of the powder 'till the whole plaister becomes a dry smooth surface——All trees cut down near the ground should have [45] the surface made quite smooth, rounding it off in a small degree as before mentioned, and the dry powder directed to be used afterwards should have an equal quantity of powdered Alabaster mixed with it, in order the better to resist the dripping of trees and heavy rains. —If any of the composition be left for a future occasion, it should be kept in a tub or other vessel, and wine of any kind poured over it, so as to cover the surface; otherwise the atmosphere will greatly hurt the efficacy of the application. — When lime rubbish of old buildings cannot be easily got, take pounded chalk, or common lime after having been slacked a month at least.— As the growth of the tree will gradually affect the plaister, by raising up its edges next the bark, care should be taken, when that happens, to rub it over with the finger, when occasion may require (which is best to be done when moistened by rain) that the plaister may be kept whole, to prevent the air and wet from

penetrating into the Wound: ——NB: Mr. For-
syth recommends pruning trees in the Spring
and beginning of summer in preference to the
Winter. —Great care should be taken to cut the
stem or branches as near as possible to some of
the last year's shoots or buds; if there be any. —
When too many shoots spring forth round the
edge of the plaister, some of them should be
rubbed off with the finger

French Pomatum

To one pound of Beef marrow, one pound of hogs
lard, one Oz. oil of Nuts or sweet oil and ¼ Oz.
Virgins Wax,[69] put it all in a bowl into boiling
Water and when melted it must be well beaten
with rods. Scent it with what Essence you
please before it is cold.

---

69. This was pure or refined wax.

[46]　**Butter**

To a peck of fine salt add one oz. of crude Sal-ammoniac[70] and two ozs. salt Peter both finely powdered mix them intimately with the fine salt—With this mixture work your butter until the buttermilk is entirely extracted then pack it salting it with the same mixed salt to such a degree as to be palatable when eat with bread and no salt. This mixture is stronger than fine salt of consequence something less is required. —This approved method of preserving the fine flavor of Butter and preventing its growing rancid was presented to the Burlington agricultural society and ordered to be published.

I have tried this method and proved very good. H.H.

NB I kept it a twelvemonth. see the next page.

To cure Beef

To every 140 lb. of Meat put 1 lb. salt petre finely powdered, 2 lb. Brown Sugar and 3 quarts fine salt mix them well together lay your Beef singly and sprinkle it all over with this mixture. let it lay ten days* then make a pickle with corse salt strong enough to bear an

---

70. Ammonium chloride.

Egg and to every twenty Gallons of this pickle add half a gallon of Lye made of hickory ashes. the pickle must be boiled and skimmed and when cold the lye put in, then pour it on the beef as it lays in the salt petre sugar and salt let it lay ten or 12 days then smoke it.

This is the receipt also for curing hams at the northward but I am convinced it would not answer in this climate tho' I have found it excellent for Beef.

Mrs. Hazzlehirst.

*N.B. The northward receipt lets it lay 3 Weeks.[71]

[47]   **Golden Cordial**

To 1 Gall. Brandy add the rinds of 4 citrons or Lemons, expose it to the sun eight days, observing to shake it each day. Then strain the Brandy from the rinds, to which add 2 lb. loaf sugar, 1 Oz. sweet Almonds 1 Oz. peach kernels, one Oz. Cinnamon and twenty five cloves, put it in the sun 8 days longer then filter it for use.

---

71. This recipe may have been obtained by Harriott during her expedition to more northern states in 1793.

Raspberry Brandy

Take 4 lb. Raspberries and 1 lb. Sugar mix them well together and let them stand all night then add 3 pints Brandy mix it well, and put it in your Jug. let it stand 8 Weeks shake it well every day then run it thro' a fine sieve for use.]72 A better way is to put 1 pint Brandy 1 lb. raspberries and ¾ lb. sugar scald them to-gether (not boil) and put them in a Jug as above.73

To preserve Butter

Take 2 lb. Salt 2 lb. Sugar and 1 lb. Salt petre beat them fine and mix well to-gether. take 1 Oz. of this mixture to every pound of Butter, work it in well and cover it close. NB. it must stand a Month before it is used.

To take the disagreeable taste from Butter made by Turnips flowers

When you skim the cream put it into boiling Water let it stand to be cold then skim it off the Water.

---

72. Harriott crossed out this passage between brackets.
73. This "better way" is spelled out on page 57.

To dry Peaches

Take cling Stone peaches, pare them and cut
them into as large thick slices as you can cut,
put them into a stew pan (say about 4 lb) pour
½ pint of Water to them and sprinkle on them
two heaped spoonsful of powderd Sugar, put
them on the fire and let them scald (but not
boil) then pour them into a sieve and let them
drain well, then spread them thin on dishes
and put them in the sun to dry, remove them on
clean dishes every day and put them in the Sun
'till they are dry. ——

x [48] Jumbles

Take the Yolks of Eight Eggs, 1 lb. Butter and 2
pnd. Sugar beat them well together then add a
sufficient quantity of flour well dried (about
) [*left blank*] to make it stiff enough to
role. then role it into Jumbles and dip each
Jumble into pounded Sugar and bake on tin
Sheets. you may add carraway seeds.

See page 43.

Bacon

Cut up the Hogs the day they are kill'd, salt them well while they are warm but do not rub them, let them lay singly on your table for the bloody brine to run off, the first day rub them well with salt and put all together in your tubs, then 2d and 3d day rub them well, the 4th day let them alone the 5th day rub well with salt Petre (2 Ozs. to a Hog) the 6th day do not touch them and let them lay till 7th or the 8th day when they must be put in Pickle made of salt and Water not boil'd that will bear an Egg it must remain in Pickle two Weeks then smoke 5 Weeks with red oak Bark. The Pickle should be boild often and must be sure to stand all night to cool before the meat is put in. Whenever the meat is taken out to rub always drain the bloody brine away. Let the Meat hang in the Smoke house a day to drain before smoking.

Mrs. McPherson

See next Page

Rice Bread—Annual Register Page 54[74]

Boil a quarter of a pound of rice 'till it is soft and well seethed. When it is cold knead it up well with ¾ lb. of wheat flour, a tea cup full of

---

74. A search through the *Annual Register* for the years 1765 to 1830 has failed to turn up this recipe.

yeast and a tea cup full of milk and a small tablespoon full of salt, let it stand 3 hours then knead it once and role it up in a hand full of flour so as to make it dry enough to put into the Oven. When baked it will produce 2 lb. of excellent white Bread.

Rice Bread

Take 4 quarts of rice beat it into flour, sift it, take one quart of the [*one word illegible*] siftings and boil it soft, spread it in your tray and while just warm put in your leaven or yeast and mix by degrees all the flour in, put it to rise and when risen which will be seen by its cracking put it into your pans and bake it. NB. it will be so soft when put in the pans that you may dip it up.

Mrs. McPherson

[49] To wash grease or paint

Put lime and salt into Water, let it stand all night, then pour it off clean and wash the floor or clothes well, then wash it off with soap and clean Water.

To fatten Oxen

Mix Rye (or rice flour) like paste leave it 3, 4, or 5 days according to the Weather to ferment and become sour then delute it with Water and thicken this Water with hay cut into chaff which they drink, you may add leaven but none give it till it becomes sour and it fattens better on account of its acidity. A large Ox will eat in this Way 22 lb. given at 3 times p. day

Young

To preserve cream

Take ½ lb. white Sugar dissolve it in the smallest possible quantity of Water when melted boil it 2 minutes in an earthen vessel then pour to it half a pint of new cream while the sugar is quite hot and when cold pour it into bottles and cork tight.

The Virginia Mode of curing Bacon[75]

For 24 Hams take 6 lb. Salt finely pounded, 3 lb. Brown Sugar or Molasses and 1 lb. salt petre mix them together and rub each Ham all over well with this mixture, and pack them down in

75. Harriott might have obtained these directions during her northern tour of 1793.

a Tub and let them so remain for 5 or 6 days then turn them and sprinkle some salt over them and so remain for 5 or 6 days longer then add to them brine or pickle strong enough to bear an Egg let them be corned with it for [*left blank*] Weeks when they will be fit to smoke. See page 54.

[50] ## Cheap Paint

Take a piece of hide about a foot square boil it well in about 10 Gallons of Water then add about a Bushel of the coarse rice flour, boil it 'till it is like starch, then strain it and put as much lime to it as will make it as white as you chuse. I generally put about a peck to this quantity, and if you find it too thick to lay it on with the brush, add a little Water to it, as you use it. In first using this mixture I generally give the buildings two coats, after that, if they are painted over once a year it will keep them perfectly white.

To wash silk stockings

Take weak Lye such as is used for washing clothes, wash the stockings in it cold very clean with soap, then soak them well, put them in clean lye and boil them 'till all the old blue comes out. then chop up some soap and put it into a pint of Lye, put it on the fire and let it boil till the soap is melted, then take it off and add to it 2 large spoonfulls of liquid blue, strain it and put in the stockings while it is scalding hot rub them well in it, then take them out and rub them again well with the hands, then let them hang in the shade 'till about half dry then mangle them. NB. a pint of Lye with 2 spoonfulls of Blue will do about 4 or 5 pair of stockings.

[51]   Another cheap paint

Take 3 parts un slacked lime
2 parts wood ashes
1 part fine sand

Put them all together and mix with lintseed oil of a proper consistence for painting—it must have 2 coats.
NB. I would first grind the ingredients with oil and then mix with oil.

To wash Carpets

Take a small tub of good soap Suds and mix with it one Beef gall then dip in a piece of woolen or a soft Brush and and [*sic*] rub well the carpet and then rince with cold water first having spread it out of doors upon smooth boards.

[*Several words illegible*] or Grey colour

Take of Maple Bark any quantity you please, of Chinkapin bark and galeberry bushes[76] one third less than of the Maple bark, boil them together till the decoction is very strong and dark, pour it off clear and put to it such a proportion of Coppres[77] as will make your dye of the shade you chuse which must be done by tryal, observing it must be always heated when you put in your cloth.

---

76. The bark of the gale (or gall) shrub was used to dye black. See *A Dictionary of Americanisms on Historical Principles,* ed. by Mitford M. Mathews (Chicago, 1951), s.v., "gall."

77. Copperas was a name long given to proto-sulphates of copper, iron and zinc. *OED,* s.v., "copperas."

To dye a good olive brown

Fill a ten gallon pot half full with the inside bark of Hiccory, fill up the pot with Water and boil it very strong, then put in a large spoonful of Allum and half a spoonful of Copperas. Without the Copperas the dye will be yellow, and in proportion as copperas is added it will be a pale or deep Olive. While boiling put in your cloth and keep it stirring for 8 or 10 Minutes, then take it out, rince it in cold water and hang it to dry.

See page 53.

[52] ## To Dye Pink

Gather Saffron while wet with the dew, pound it well in a Mortar, and mix it well in rain Water in a large Pewter or Earthen Vessel and let it stand in the Sun. Wet your Linen or Cotton in warm soap suds made of Castile Soap then put it in the Dye and let it remain in three or four hours, then wash it well in cold pump Water which will turn it to a fine pink colour, hang it in the shade to dry, and if the colour is not deep enough, dip it as often as you please in the same way. Be sure to use Castile Soap and never heat the dye but in the Sun.

Milk Paint

Take 6 oz. of Slack'd lime, rub it up with a small quantity of skim Milk, then add more milk to make the quantity mix'd with the lime one pint. add 6 oz. of boil'd Lintseed oil gradually, mixing it well with the lime and milk, pour on 3 pints more of milk stiring well the Mixture then crumble on the surface 5 lb. of Spanish White (Whiting) which will sink by degrees then work up the whole Mass well with a wooden Spatula.

NB. The Milk must be skim milk but not the least sour.

Strong Cement

Take plaister of Paris Ground very fine and put into an Iron pot, put it on the fire and keep it boiling at least half an hour or longer then take it up and when cold put it by for use in a Bll. or box. When it is used mix it with cold Water and lay it on as quick as possible with your Trowel. it should be laid on about ½ In. thick.

[53] A good green paint

For the 1st. coat (after priming) Take Mineral green ground in oil yellow Ocre and white lead in do. mixed with boil'd oil and spirit of Turpentine and Varnish. For the varnish melt 4 lb. rosin and mix with 2 quarts spirit Turpentine. in the 2d. coat of green paint put no white lead and but ¼ yellow Ocre ground in oil.

good Olive Brown to dye Cambricks etc.

Take one third hiccory and 2 thirds Maple (the inner barks) boil them very strong like strong Coffee strain it and dissolve in it as much Copperas as will make it of the colour you like, the more coperas the darker. Treat your cloth, shake it well but do not wring it put it into the dye boiling hot and keep it stiring all the time it is in (say about a quarter of an hour then rince it in cold water and lay it to dry as quick as possible in the Sun, if the colour is not dark enough heat your dye and dip it again as before. Never wring it but shake, stretch and hang it   See page 59.[78]

---

78. This is an error. Page 51 was intended.

Cement for fruit trees or others

Take ¾ chalk ¼ Tar mix them well together and boil slow 'till of consistence of soft Wax lay on the trees with a hot trowel as soon as you cut off a limb.

For Bugs

1 Oz. Corrosive Sublimate in a quart Bottle of Turpentine.

[54]   **For making Bacon**

Cut up the hogs the day they are killed, and then salt them well (but do not rub them) with a peck of salt to each hog, the next day take 2 lb. Sugar and ¼ lb. Salt petre to *each Hog* and a little more salt added to what salt hangs about them mix it all together and rub well with it particularly Hams or legs put them all in a Tub together and let them lie three days (if the weather is very cold they may lie a day or two longer) then take them out of the tubs and rub them well with salt alone and put them back in the tubs with the bloody brine from which you took them and let them lie Eight days longer, then take them out pour away all the brine or pickle from them and rub them a third time with the salt that is unmelted about them and a little more added and about ½ pint of red pepper powderd let them then remain in the tubs two weeks then smoke them till they are well dried making in the whole less than a Month from the killing to the smoking them. The hogs I cured were very large. Mrs. Martin says she rubs with the salt Petre and Sugar all round then begins and rub with salt and puts them altogether in the Tubs.

[55] Mr. Daniels method of curing Bacon in Virginia

Hogs should not weigh more than 120 lbs.—When you cut them up do *not* take out the hip bone and never cut a slit by the hock and do not touch them with salt Peter.

Take a bushel of Salt *moderately* finely pounded (not too fine) add to it ½ gall: Molasses, and ½ Gallon hiccory Ashes, mix it all well to-gether and rub your meat well with it puting the hams by themselves. When they are well rub'd put them in tubs with the Skin down, and put on some of the Mixture on the hams as you lay them in, pack them close in your tubs and never touch them again 'till you hang them up to smoke when they should be rub'd over with a thin coat of the same mixture. They must lie from 4 to 5, 6, or 7 Weeks according to the Weather and should be smoked 10 days or a fortnight, then take them down lay them on shelves and when dry pack them away.—It will take about a peck of Salt to each hog of this size. Mr. Danial says they never kill hogs after the middle of January.

Sausages

x

Mrs. Motte

To 15 lb. Meat (9 lb. lean to 6 lb. fat.) pickd and chopd fine put ½ pint Salt one Table Spoonful Salt Peter finely pounded—2 Table Spoonsfull dried sage and 2 spoonful dried Thyme finely pounded, 1 handful green parsely chop'd fine ½ pepper ¼ All spice 1 Nutmeg and a pinch of Mace pounded all fine Season the Meat and let it lay all night and stuff them in the Morning. NB the Skin should be scraped very thin and every little film taken off.

[56]   ## Vinegar[79]

Take 10 lb. coarse Sugar and as many gallons of Water, boil them together as long as any Scum will rise and skim it well, then put it into Tubs and when about half cold put in a thick slice of toasted bread well soak'd with yeast, let it work in the tubs 24 hours then put it in Jugs.

NB I find it must stand a year before fit for use and is very good.

---

79. This vinegar recipe is a brief and somewhat differently worded version of the one on p. 11. It is later than the other, and it lacks the details relative to storing the vinegar.

To pickle Onions

Take large Onions put them into strong salt
and Water for 48 hours then put them in the
Sun with a thin cloth over them and let them
stand a day till the Water is evaporated then
boil some strong Vinegar with a good deal of
spice and pour over them boiling hot, cover
them close and they are fit to eat as soon as
cold.

To pickle Mushrooms White

First boil 3 quarts of White Vinegar with a
handful of allspice 3 raw ginger cut (not beat)
small and a little mace cover it close and let it
boil ¼ of an hour, let it stand to be cold and
keep it to pour over the Mushrooms; put the
bits of ginger and mace in the bottles. Peel
Mushroom buttons, and with a knife gently
scrape the top like [one word illegible] is [one
word illegible] yellow. Wash them clean in cold
Water then put them in a stew pan sprinkle a
little salt over them, cover them close and put
them on a very slow fire, in a very few minutes
there will be a liquor, take it off and shake it
well, thro' them out of the pan pour off the liquor let them cool and then squeeze them well
in a thin cloth 'till they are quite dry then put
them thus dry into clean bottles and pour the
vinegar over them and as they imbibe the vinegar fill them up from time to time.

[57] ## Spruce Beer

Take a pint of Sassafras root cut up small and one handful of spruce pine, a small peice of china root 2 spoonsfull of rough rice and 2 spoonsfull of corn and 1 quart of Molasses. Put these ingredients with some grounds of Beer into a 3 Gall. Jug, fill it with *cold* Water in the Morning and at night bottle it off: If the weather is Warm it will be fit to drink at noon.

Very good

Plumb Brandy

Take the August plumbs *quite ripe* cut them round by making a circular incision through the Skin and pulp to the stone. fill your Vessel with them and cover them with Brandy. after they have been in Brandy six Weeks pour it off and sweeten it to your taste.

Raspberry Brandy

Take 1 lb. Raspberries 1 pint Brandy ¾ lb. Sugar Scald them together (not boil) and put it in your jug, let it stand 8 Weeks (not more and strain it off.

Orange flower syrup[80]

Journey cake[81]

Take a pint of Hominy cold mash it and mix well with a gill fine flower then mix 6 Spoonsfull of milk and spread it on your board and spread a little milk over it as you put it down to bake. This quantity for 2 middlesized Journey cakes. When rice is used it should be boild very soft and let stand to cool and mix as above.

Rice Milk

Take ½ pint rice put it in a quart Sauce pan and fill it with Water, let it boil stiring it often till the rice is quite soft indeed almost dissolved like starch then put in a quart of Milk and let boil together till about as thick as a pap then put it in your dish and in a few minutes it will look like cream.

---

80. See next to last recipe.

81. Journey cakes had gained their name in the British Isles where they had served travelers both as a quick food available at inns and for eating along the way. In Britain these hearth cakes were made of oatmeal or barley, but in America corn was the usual ingredient. In this recipe Harriott offers rice as an alternative grain. See William Woys Weaver (ed.), *A Quaker Woman's Cookbook: The Domestic Cookery of Elizabeth Ellicott Lea* (Philadelphia, 1982), pp. xxxvi, lxiv.

[58] Charlotte à la façon de Mr. Short.[82]

Rub some butter over the pan first.—Then cover the inside of the pan with thin slices of stale bread well buttered. Next shake a little *brown* sugar all over the bread. Now begin with the apples. Cover the bread and sugar which was first laid over the pan, with apples sliced thin, then shake a handful of brown sugar over the apples, then a handful or two of grated bread all over the sugar, then small bits of butter all over the grated bread. Then shake either powdered Cinnamon or nutmeg all over the butter. And so you go on beginning again with the apples and finishing with the cinnamon or nutmeg until the pan is full enough to put into the oven. When you find it shrinking in the middle that is a sign of its being done. It requires a great deal of baking and the oven must not be too hot.——

---

82. This recipe was inserted by a hand different from that of Harriott Horry. There is good reason to suppose that the source of this recipe was William Short (1759–1849), the very able diplomat and lifelong friend of Jefferson. Short spent many years in Paris between 1784 and 1810 before returning to the United States to live in Philadelphia. Here Harriott could have met him in 1815 when she spent nine days in that city. See *Dictionary of American Biography,* 9:128–29; Harriott Horry, Journal, 1815, SCHS.

[59] **For Dying Blue**

Take 24 Galls. rain Water free from grease or dirt and put into it 4 lb. copras and 4 lb. stone lime. Take 2 lb. Indigo grind it as fine as possible (adding rain Water to it till you have a quart or 3 pints of the Indigo and Water) it must be quite an impalpable powder. then put it in a Bll. with the other ingredients and churn it up 3 times a day till you see a foam on the top of a changable colour and the dye of a dark green streak'd with black then let it stand 2 days to settle. Boil the yarn so as to be thoroughly Wet,* wring it very hard dip it in the dye about half the depth of the Baul turning it over the hands three or four times observing never to let it go to the bottom among the grounds wring it and hang it up till you go over the yarn 2 or 3 times a day. When the yarn quits turning green it will dye no more set it with Vitriol and Water made sour enough to drink then rince it thro' one or two Waters— When the dye grow too weak you may put in ½ of each of the above quantities of Indigo, Stone lime and copras and a bit of allum the size of an Egg but this quantity will dye near 200 hanks before it becomes too weak to use.

Mrs. Robinson

[one or two words illegible]

*Mrs. Holmes says should be ½ lb. Allum in this Water

[60]   To wash woolen yarn

The Wool should *not* be washd but spun with
the natural grease then wash the yarn in cold
rain or river Water two or three times without
soap 'till the grease which will lather is out,
then wash it well with Soap and cold Water and
it will be quite White. NB it should never touch
hot Water from the first or after it is [*one word
illegible*].

[The following four recipes are on loose slips of paper. The untitled recipe for rum punch is in Harriott's hand. Those for syllabub and orange flower syrup were written by someone else, and that for kitchen pepper by a third person. The orange flower syrup recipe was probably intended for inclusion on page 57 where the title alone appears.]

[A rum punch]

The peel of 8 Oranges and 8 Lemons in 1 quart of rum. 3 Gallons of Water boild with 3 lb. of loaf Sugar and the Whites of 8 Eggs. 2 and ¾ pints of orange juice and 1 and ¾ Pints of Lemon juice. strain the quart of rum from the Peel and add one Gallon more of rum to rest of the ingredients.

To make Solid Syllabub, a nice dessert.

1 pint of cream ½ pint of wine. The juice of one lemon sweetened to your taste. Put it in a wide mouthed bottle—a quart bottle will answer. Shake it for ten minutes. Pour it into your glasses. It must be made the evening before it is to be used.——

Orange flower syrup

Stir 9 pounds of loaf sugar into 6 quarts of water (cold) Put this sweetened water on the fire and boil into a syrup Skim it well. Then put into it as it boils half a pound of the leaves of Orange flowers. Let it continue to boil till the flowers are shrivelled and the strength and sweetness of them seem to be extracted. Then strain it through a cloth Squeeze it well and bottle the syrup.

Kitchen Pepper[83]

One ounce of Ginger—pepper cinnamon cloves and Nutmeg half an ounce of each—6 ounces of salt Mix it well keep it dry. its excellent in all brown Sauces.

---

83. Mixtures of spices had existed since the late medieval period, at times even made by merchants to sell. By the late seventeenth or eighteenth centuries they became known as "kitchen pepper." See Wilson, *Food and Drink,* pp. 284, 294.

Index

Hampton Plantation

The eighteenth-century plantation house, Hampton, the home of Daniel and Harriott Pinckney Horry, is located in Hampton Plantation State Park a short distance off U.S. Highway 17 and about 40 miles north of Charleston and 20 miles south of Georgetown.

It was in this beautiful home, which looks as it did during the lifetime of Harriott, that she and her mother, Eliza Lucas Pinckney, entertained George Washington in 1791, and Harriott entertained Lafayette in 1825 during his American tour. For a time in the present century, Hampton was the home of the late Archibald Rutledge, poet laureate of South Carolina.

The plantation grounds can be visited every day during daylight hours, but to see the interior of the mansion, which has restricted visiting hours, it is necessary to make arrangements with the park superintendent.